Rush and Leafcraft

Overleaf
Tom Metcalfe harvesting rushes at St Ives
Huntingdon

Rush and Leafcraft

Germaine Brotherton

Houghton Mifflin Company Boston
1977

This book is dedicated to Evelyn Low, who
gave me a first appreciation of crafts, and
time to work at them

First American Edition
Copyright ©1977 by Germaine Brotherton

ISBN 0-395-25787-5   6-20-97

Printed in Great Britain

10 9 8 7 6 5 4 3 2 1

Contents

Acknowledgement

Acknowledgments are due to the following people and organisations who donated articles or allowed them to be photographed:
Elsevier International Limited
The British Museum: cosmetic box (27), sandal (51); *Home and Country* (1); The Hand Crafts Advisory Association: Mexican doll (14); Mrs A Bristow: woven mat (49); Mrs C Kendzior: embroidery on net (41); Miss P Lawrence: linen basket (33); Mrs K Whitbourn: miniature log basket (8); and to Mr N Russell for taking the photograph of his Orkney chair. I should like to thank all the friends who took the trouble to gather plant material for me to use, Alan Sander for the many photographic sessions which he willingly undertook, and Graham Murrell for the jacket photograph.

I am grateful to the Women's Institute Movement for the opportunities it provides to learn the different crafts and I am especially indebted to the many people who have given so generously of their craft knowledge, in particular Mr J Dunwell, Mrs N Kimmins and Mrs K Whitbourn. The frontispiece is reproduced by kind permission of *Home and Country*.

My grateful thanks to Barbara Siedlecka for her advice on drawing the diagrams, and lastly to my husband for his cooperation and sound criticism.

G B
Orpington, Kent 1977

Introduction

A craftsman who is able to gather the raw material for the craft from the garden or neighbouring countryside, before turning it into articles which are both useful and beautiful, has a double satisfaction.

For hundreds of years rushes and irises have been used for floor coverings, at first strewn loosely on the floor and renewed every summer, later plaited and sewn into carpets. They have been used for seating chairs and making baskets for many different purposes, such as cradles, workmen's tool baskets, and hassocks, which were all in common use in the nineteenth century.

However, more recently, with the much greater ease of transport, craft materials from all over the world have been generally available, while local ones are often neglected. This is a pity, not only because so much is wasted that might be of use, but also because we are more likely to have a basic, if possibly hazy, background knowledge of the best way to use local plants, built up of things seen in use, perhaps in the country, or preserved in homes or museums, or read about in books, or even just mentioned by elderly relatives. We find too that many imported materials have alien techniques applied to them which fail to do them justice, as, for example, cane is often used in ways which are better suited to willow.

Starting with the traditional ways of using rushes and leaves, it will be easy to see some of the possibilities, and from there to be drawn to explore other ideas worth developing. There are many different plants which can be used in the ways to be described, which probably fall into one of the following groups:

1 GARDEN LEAVES of a strap-like or linear nature. However large or small, any leaves of this type are useful, such as crocus, daffodil, iris, montbretia, crocosmia, hemerocallis and gladiolus.

2 RUSHES are found in slow-moving rivers or near the edge of ponds. The bulrush, *scirpus lacustris* or Cooper's rush (from its use between the staves of wooden barrels to prevent leaking) grows up to 2.5 m ($2\frac{3}{4}$ yd) long, but the size and texture of the plant varies a great deal with the type of water and soil in which it happens to be growing.

3 REED MACE, *typha latifolia*, grows in shallow water with long, beautifully flat, even leaves. It has solid dark brown flower spikes often mistakenly called bulrushes.

4 SEDGE, *carex*, is common on watersides and wet moors; it has tough, three-sided stems and leaves which may have a cutting edge.

5 GRASSES are usually supple enough for both leaves and stems to be used. Marram grass is a tough, useful species growing in sand dunes. Pampas grass has a long, strong leaf but needs to be used with great care because of its extremely cutting surface.

6 MAIZE, although rather short and wide, the sheath of white leaves close to the corn cob is soft and supple and the light colour can be a useful contrast to other material. The leaves themselves should be used before they get too tough.

It is worth trying other plants with leaves which are wider than most of those mentioned so far, because you may find that they work up quite well. The best thing to do is to search for whatever might possibly be useful and is available within your reach, whether in the garden or the countryside. Gather some, dry it, and try out a technique which seems most suitable. At the same time, note how the plant varies as the season progresses. It may be, for example, that an unexpected change of colour happens in the autumn of which you might wish to take advantage another year. When the leaves and rushes dry they will shrink considerably, so gather as much as you can store. The material costs nothing except the time spent collecting it, but it is important to get to know its character, and that knowledge will only come through working with it and experimenting.

The aim of this book is to suggest ways of using these materials and to explain the methods and techniques involved, rather than to give detailed instructions for many specific articles. The principal ways of using them are for plaiting, weaving, seating and coiling, but they can also be knotted, used as a veneer, and turned into paper, amongst other possibilities. Once you have worked through some of the basic techniques and got to know the variety of character of different plants, you will want to try out your own ideas.

1 Gathering, storing and preparation of material

GATHERING

The best time to collect leaves and rushes is usually when the plants are fully grown, after that they may begin to harden or deteriorate, but leaves may be left until later in the year if you prefer their autumn colouring and they are still in good condition. Crocus and daffodil leaves will be ready in the spring, rushes in June or July, and gladioli may be left until the corms are lifted in October; so harvesting can be well spread out through the year.

Choose a dry day for harvesting and cut the full length of the leaves. If the plants are growing in a lake or river, cut under water as low as possible because the strongest part is the base, or butt end. The leaves may be almost non-existent and the plant consist of clumps of cylindrical stems ending in little tufts of flower heads at, or near, the tip. These stems are often filled with a continuous white pith which used to be soaked in tallow and used as lamp wicks. A flat-bottomed boat is a help in collecting large quantities – try not to bend the rushes as this usually creates a weakness. Tie up the material in bundles, remembering that they will shrink a great deal and need to be retied later on.

DRYING

If many bundles have been gathered they can be dried outside, leaning against each other like sheaves of corn, or spread out against a support which will allow the wind to blow through, but they should be brought under cover if it rains. The sun will bleach away much of the colour, so to keep them green, dry out of direct sunlight, in the dark if possible. A barn, loft or garage would be ideal as there must be room for the air to circulate. For small quantities, an airing cupboard is useful, or they can be laid out on the floor or on top of cupboards, on newspaper, and turned frequently. The main thing is to prevent mould forming. The time needed depends on the drying temperature and the thickness of the plants and may be anything from a few hours to two to three weeks.

STORING

When the material feels much lighter and if, when you bend it, it sounds papery, it should be ready for storing. Bundle the stuff up again and keep it in an airy place till needed. Do not wrap it up or put it in a container, as air needs to circulate to prevent mould from developing. It should be out of direct sunlight and in an atmosphere which is not too hot, as this can make rushes and leaves very brittle. Two hooks in the rafters will hold several bundles of long material out of the way and they should remain usable for years.

Keep different types of leaves in different bundles, and if rushes are roughly sorted into bundles of thick, medium and thin sizes it will save time when work starts later on.

1   Some of the materials used, showing differences of size, colour and texture

PREPARATION

Do not use the material dry as it will crack every time it is bent. It has to be damped and given time to mellow. This does not mean soaking it for a long time, which only waterlogs and weakens it, but just a dip in and out of water – rainwater if possible – or laying it on the grass and watering it. Wrap it in a cloth, or sacking, or a sheet of plastic. The latter is good for controlling the spread of dampness but it keeps the bundle airless so that it will heat up quicker than in a cloth wrapping. Keep the bundle out of the sun and wind, and, when working, only uncover a little of the butt ends, select the size needed and draw it out, leaving the bundle intact so that it does not dry out. The mellowing time depends on the thickness of the material, it may be half an hour for thin leaves or overnight for thick rushes, but it also depends on the atmosphere – on a misty autumn day thin rushes may only need wiping with a wet cloth to make them pliable, while after a spell of hot summer weather leaves may need to be mellowed for several hours before they will bend without cracking. It is very much a question of trial and error and being guided by previous experience.

Try to damp only what will be used in a days work, as the remainder should then be dried off to prevent spots of mould forming, particularly in hot weather. Before using, wipe each leaf or rush firmly with a damp cloth or sponge, this removes any dust or mud and also air from the pith of rushes. If you can fold them over without hearing a papery rustle, they should be in good condition for working. In fact it is no exaggeration to say that a mellow fresh-water English bulrush should feel like a satin ribbon.

TOOLS

In general you will need:
  Scissors
  Ruler or tape measure
  Cloth or plastic sheets for wrapping up
  Rags or plastic sponge for wiping
  Old rolling pin (or straight sided bottle)
  or wooden mallet for pressing
  Football lacing awl (obtainable in a
  sports shop) for threading away stakes, etc
  Packing needles of various sizes
  Soft string
In addition: for thick plaiting: a sailor's
  palm (a thimble would be dangerous)
  For seating: a packing stick to insert the
  padding
  For baskets: various moulds preferably
  of wood or pottery, which grip the
  work better than glass or plastic.
  A wrapped brick or other weight, useful
  as a third hand to hold down stakes to
  begin with.
  For knotting: a fid, which is a long
  tapering cone, or a substitute such as a
  meat skewer.
  For intricate cutting: a Swanley knife or
  Swann-Morton craft tool, which are
  useful small knives with very pointed
  blades.

The different methods of working can be treated independently – it is not necessary to plait before weaving or coiling, for example, but it is necessary to get to know the material by practising on a simple article in whichever method you decide on. So before starting on a basket it is much better to make one or two mats to become familiar with the basic technique without too many complications.

Finally, a word of warning: you may need to have a blind faith in the attractive possibilities of your dried plants, because leaves gathered in summer with high hopes may, in the middle of winter, look like nothing more than second rate cattle fodder. Don't be misled. After selecting, preparing, and above all with firm, smooth, rhythmic and sympathetic handling of the leaves or rushes the results can be unexpectedly beautiful.

2 *Oval plaited mat with scroll centre.*
Rush
3 *Reverse of the same mat*

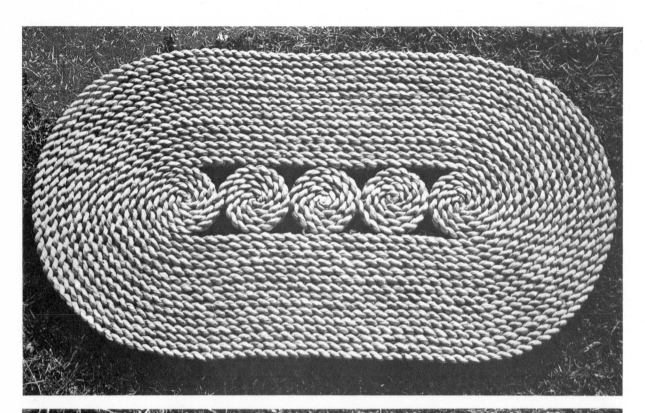

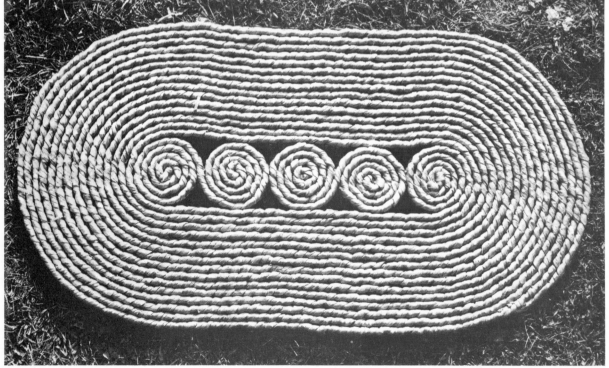

2 Plaiting

Some leaves or rushes taken individually may be very strong, but others are weak, and only gain their strength and usefulness from the different ways of combining them. A simple way is to plait them and sew up the plait. Most people, at one time or another, have worked a hair plait with three groups of strands, so that the technique is basically a familiar one. It is also an easy way of using material of any length and different thicknesses, because you can keep joining in new lengths as often as you wish, to keep the combined elements grouped in plaiting strands of uniform thickness. The plaits can be sewn up in various ways to produce flat or three-dimensional articles, or they can be worked into decorative or useful knots, small or large. The plaiting can be done on any scale – crocus leaves and some varieties of iris can be made into a fine plait 3 mm ($\frac{1}{8}$ in.) wide for key guards or neck ornaments, while bunches of 15 rushes or leaves will work into a plait 3 or 4 cm ($1\frac{1}{2}$ or 2 in.) wide suitable for a log basket the method of making the plait, however, can be just the same.

There are many different plaits and the following are a selection from several types. They can be roughly divided into two groups: flat, plaited braids, and solid or tubular plaits.

FLAT PLAITS

(a) 3 plait   *(photographs 2, 3, 6, 7, 8, 9)*
Tie up a bundle of rushes or leaves very firmly by the butt ends, 6 or 9 for a first sample and hang them from a convenient hook, or any place which will allow you to work under tension. Divide the bundle into three groups which feel equal, 2 on the right and one on the left, which we will now call strands, and start plaiting by laying the outside one of the pair, A, across its neighbour B, to lie in the centre alongside C. There are now 2 strands on the left, so take the outside one C, over A and lay it in the centre alongside B. Continue working from side to side in this way, keeping the angle between the single strand and the pair of strands wide open, to make a close, firm plait.

The leaves making up a strand may be folded over or twisted into a coil, so try a

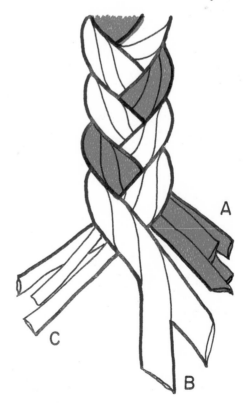

DIAGRAM 1
3 plait

15

sample length using three different methods, to see which suits you best:

1 Twist each strand away from the centre before placing it across the centre strand. This will give a rope like edge.

2 Fold each strand inward as you move it across. This gives a smooth edge to the plait.

3 Twist each group to the right all the time, if you are right-handed, and work with that hand while holding the plait with the left, this gives one rope-like edge and one smooth edge, so one side of a mat would look different to the other (photographs 2 and 3). To smooth out a plait, roll it while still damp.

JOINS   As soon as a strand begins to feel thin, add a new butt by pushing the end to the back in the centre of the plait, before gathering it up with the rest of the strand. An even neater join is done by hiding the new butt between the leaves already in the strand, but you will need to watch that it does not get pulled out during subsequent movements. The important thing is to see that the ends are in the middle of the plait, not at an edge, so that when the plait is sewn up they will not be seen, and they should all be on the same side, so that the plait has a right and a wrong side.

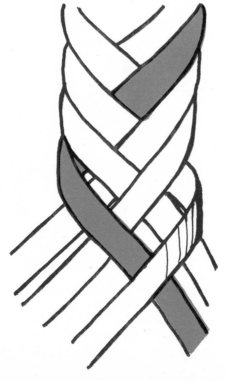

DIAGRAM 2
Grecian plait

16

(b) Grecian plait

This looks rather like a smoother, thicker 3 plait and feels comfortable for a handle. Using 5 (or 7) strands, fold the outside strand over 2 (or 3) towards the centre, in the same way as a three plait, but slightly overlapping each time to give a smoothly rounded edge.

(c) Drawn up 3 plait

This is suitable for a small handle on a lid as it produces a good width from 2 thin rushes. If using leaves, they should be supple. Fold the 2 strands over a string, very much closer to the tips than the butts, tie and hang up. Tie the ends of the tips together and use them as one strand, then make seven movements of a 3 plait, folding evenly towards the centre but not too tightly. Hold the knotted tips firmly, and gently slide the plait up close, which will give it quite a different, wider look. Continue in the same way, plaiting and then pushing up on the same strand, making sure that the folds are even in length, to keep the plait even in width (photograph 17).

(d) Flat woven plaits

This family of plaits will give flat braids, narrow or wide, in a simple 'over one, under one' weave, or a variety of combinations of short and long strokes. For these, the width of each strand, as well as its thickness, needs to be kept even. To join in new lengths, overlap the new and old strand for several movements. Use material that is the same width for most of its length – rushes or reed mace leaves for example – or be prepared to use more than one element in a strand to be able to control its width.

THE 5 PLAIT   This is a useful example, and an easy one to start with. Tie up 5 strands, number them from left to right, keep 1 and 2 on the left and 3, 4, 5 on the right. Fold 5 over 4 and weave under 3. Fold 1 over 2 and weave under 5. Renumber the strands from the left and repeat. As usual the angle between the groups should be kept wide open, and aim at forming square shapes rather than long diamonds. Fold the edges over rather than bending them round, so that if two plaits are sewn together side by side, the ladder stitches will disappear within the folds.

Any odd number of strands can be used in the same way, if you want a wider braid. An even number of strands is worked in the same way except at the edges – one side folds over, while the other side will have to fold under to keep the pattern going.

Shaping a curve into a flat plait: to make a bend to the left, work with the right hand strands only, weaving each across until all are pointing to the left, except one. This will be the centre of the curve, so fold it over (or under, as the case may be) and weave it right across, then turn the whole plait anti-clockwise so that all the strands are now pointing to the right except the last one. Weave half the number of strands on the right, over to the left, and you will be back to a normal grouping.

These braids can be varied at the edge by allowing one or two strands to twist, or make an extra little pattern, before returning into the normal plaiting movement.

The texture can be changed, as in weaving, by repeating movements of different lengths – for example, with 7 strands, taking the outer strand over one and under two, each time. The more strands you are using, the greater the number of possibilities.

SPLICING A 5 PLAIT   This join is invisible if properly done, but it needs a little practice. Start by overlapping the ends for 15 cm (6 in.) and tie them temporarily together with string across the middle. Tidy the rushes of one end into their working position, and they should be lying over other rushes in the same direction in the plait below. Thread in the two outside stakes to follow the sequence, as they are usually the easiest to see clearly, then do the rest of the stakes in that plait and continue to follow the pattern for 6 or 8 cm (3 or 4 in.). Turn the plaits over and undo the other end until it is back to the threaded in section and then repeat as for the first plait. If, as is likely in a handle, the rushes are double in the plait, cut out the weak one of each pair and weave away the strong one. Trim the ends closely.

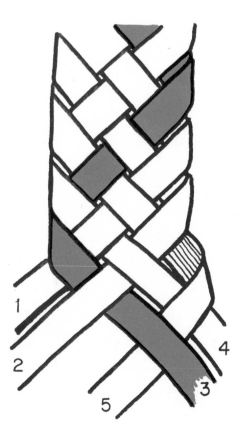

DIAGRAM 3
5 plait

(e) Tyrolean or hat plait

A decorative plait which curves easily. To get to the plaiting position, fold one strand 1, 2, into a V, lay the other strand 3, 4, through the V, fold 4 over 2, to the left, then fold 3 under 1 and over 4 to the right. This forms a second V inside the first, and every time 2 strands have been moved they will form a new V in the centre. Move each strand as follows: fold 1 behind 4 and 3, over 2 and out to the right, horizontally, then weave it under 2 and over 3 to lie beside 4. Repeat from the right with strand 2 behind 3 and 1, over 4 and out. Keep the folds very close and firm. If necessary, this plait can be eased round into a very close circle, and sewn to itself, in the way that hats were often made, or used as an edging for a plainer article.

FORMING A CORNER: (to turn to the right) When a left hand strand has been moved across to its horizontal position, pointing to the right, leave it there, take the strand now on the left, over one and under one, to lie above the first. Turn the plait round to the left so that the new V is in the working position, and start plaiting from the right. For a sharper corner, weave twice more to the right, which shifts the V further round, before starting to plait again.

4 Tyrolean plait used as an edging. The centre is made up of short linked loops, each covering 4 squares. Maize

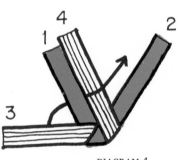

DIAGRAM 4
Tyrolean plait

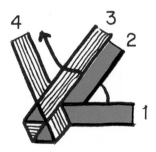

DIAGRAM 5
Tyrolean plait

TUBULAR PLAITS

These can be worked on their own, or round a core, either to cover the core, or to make the plait thicker.

(a) Round plait

Tie up 4 strands and fan them out, with 2 on the left and 2 on the right. Take the left hand strand round the back, bring it up between the right hand strand and its neighbour, and lay it over one strand, towards the left. We are now back to 2 strands on the left and 2 on the right, so take the right hand strand round the back, bring it up between the left hand strand and its neighbour, and lay it over one strand, towards the right. Repeat from the beginning. In this and the following plait the stakes need to be kept carefully in position, particularly in the middle, as the sequence is easy to lose. While still damp it can be rolled smooth on the table with the palm of the hand, and it can either be worked with fairly flat strands, or groups of leaves twisted into a rope-like coil as you work.

TO WORK OVER A CORE: each strand, as it goes round the back, goes behind the core, and then in front of it, as it is laid across the centre.

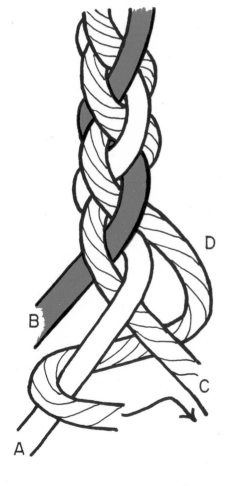

DIAGRAM 6
Round plait

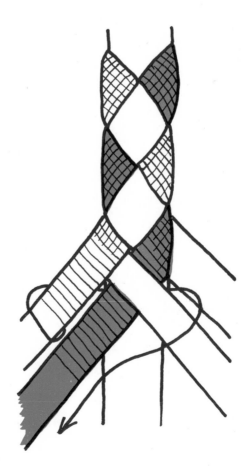

DIAGRAM 7
Round plait over a core

19

(b) Square plait

This is worked on the same principle as the round plait but with more strands to manage. Tie up 8 strands, spread out 4 on the left and 4 on the right, and number them from the left. Take the left hand strand (1) round the back, bring it up two strands away from the other end (between 6 and 7) and lay it over two strands (5 and 6) across the centre. Re-number the strands from right, and repeat from the other side. The outside strands will soon fan out onto a higher level, the ones to watch carefully are the four in the middle.

If each side of the finished plait is flattened by rolling, or beating with a mallet, it will be quite square, but if it is worked over a core it will easily take a round shape.

TO COVER A THICK CORE: work with 2 or more strands as one unit.

(c) Fill the gap plaits

These give a more open, linked look, rather than a close weave. Tie up 7 strands, but work upwards instead of down, with the tied ends between the second and third finger of the left hand, and the strands spread out on the palm, in a circle with one vacant space. Working clockwise, lay one strand over the next two and into the gap, miss the next strand, pick up the following one and lay it over two into the new gap. Repeat.

With 9 strands you can work over 3 and into the gap, with 11, over 4 and into the gap, and so on. You can also use more than one gap, and pass more than one strand, to produce different linked plaits.

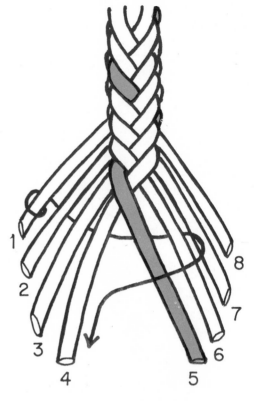

DIAGRAM 8
Square plait

DIAGRAM 9
Fill the gap plait

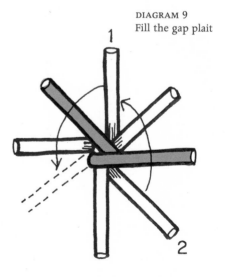

(d) Crown sinnets

Usually worked with 4 strands but can be done by any number. Working upwards, each strand in turn passes over its neighbour, but the circle is completed each time by threading the last strand under the first. Draw up all the loops evenly. The sequence may be worked continuously one way, or clockwise one round and anti-clockwise the next. This is often done quite loosely with palm leaves for Easter ornaments – some stiff fresh iris leaves such as *stylosa* can be used in the same way (photograph 5). Pulled up tightly, with rounded strands, it will give more bulk than a round plait.

ROPE

Hang up a bunch of leaves, divide into 2 equal groups, twist the right hand group towards the right, cross it over to the left and change each group to the other hand. Repeat, after pulling the groups out to a wide angle in order to keep a short, firm stroke.

This can be worked in the same way, but with 3 groups, for 3 strand rope. (Photograph 38.)

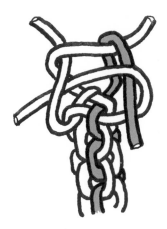

DIAGRAM 10
Crown sinnet

5 *Figure of eight knot, crown sinnets and 'fill the gap' plait. Iris stylosa and common rush*

USING PLAITS

(a) Handles
Because of their strength, plaits and rope are used for basket handles. This can be done in two different ways: either by threading the strands into the basket, making the length of plait necessary for the handle, and threading away the ends back into the basket again (photographs 15 and 17), or by making a plait into a long oval by joining it, and laying it under the basket and up the sides before it forms the handles. This will carry a greater weight with less strain on the basket itself. (Photographs 8 and 16.)

(b) Knots
The plaits can be woven into various types of knots, flat, for mats or pendants, turk's heads for rings or knobs and many others (photographs 35, 36, 40 and Chapter 8).

(c) Sewing up
Sewn up plaiting will give strong, if some-times rather heavy baskets and mats. Use a needle with a curved point, and a sailor's palm if the plait is thick or tough. The string should be soft and strong – such as fillis, or garden twine of a colour to blend with the plait, and of a suitable thickness. The needle will pass through more easily if the plait is dry. It you need extra pressure use a sailors palm, not a thimble.

TO SEW UP A ROUND MAT: if the plait was not started by folding over the first strands, wrap the beginning very firmly several times with the end of the sewing string before stabbing through it, and trimming the ends closely. Fold the plait into a tight coil, right side outside, and stab through the middle of several thick-nesses. A right handed worker will find it easier to coil anti-clockwise. The stitches never go over the edge of the plait, where they would show, so continue to coil, and stitch through the middle of the plait and the middle of the previous row, together, the needle always re-entering on the same side as its exit. To join in a new length of string, tie it with a sheet band to the old end, and continue sewing (diagram 13) On the last round, if the stitches are care-fully taken as short strokes between the strands, they will sink into the plait and disappear. The end of the plait is gradually flattened by leaving out some leaves and the remaining ends threaded in to follow the previous row.

DIAGRAM 12
Sewing up a round mat

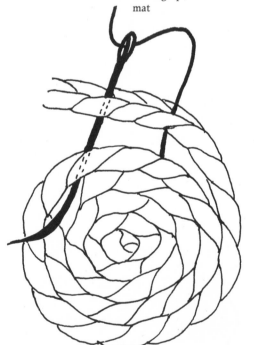

DIAGRAM 11
Sailor's palm

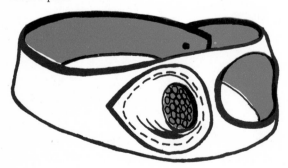

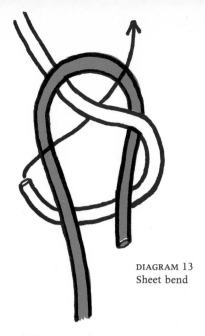

DIAGRAM 13
Sheet bend

SQUARE OR RECTANGULAR MAT   Start the centre as in diagram 15, and as corners tend to round off, pinch them well into shape every time you reach one.

VARIATIONS   An open work band is often done by working the plait into a wave. A triangular wooden shape can be used as a gauge – the plait is fitted round it, sewn together, then the gauge is turned the other way up and the plait fitted again. Or the shaping can be done round headless nails knocked into a board.

If in doubt about the length of plait needed, sew it up before cutting off the ends of the plait, then they can always be redamped to lengthen it if necessary.

SCROLL   Mark the middle of a plait about 1 m (1 yd) long and sew up one end like a mat until it reaches the middle; start again from the other end, coil the opposite way, in an S bend, and sew up till the 2 circles meet, where one or two stitches will keep them together.

If scrolls are wanted as a decoration near the edge of a round mat, it is easier to join them all into a circle and then sew up the solid centre until it fits, rather than the other way round.

OVAL MAT   It can be started with a long straight line down the centre or with scrolls. For the latter, after joining up the scrolls, start sewing up the main length of plait as if for a round mat until it reaches the size of a half scroll, sew it to the scrolls and then continue sewing round the whole group until the mat is the size you need.

DIAGRAM 15
Starting a square mat

DIAGRAM 16
Wave type decoration

DIAGRAM 14
Starting an oval mat

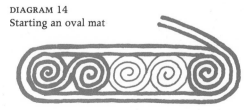

DIAGRAM 17
Wrought iron idea for
pattern

6   Spanish basket. Iris and maize

The spanish basket (photograph 6) is made up of a round base and 4 flower-like side sections of maize, edged and joined with rows of plaited iris, which continue up to form the handles.

Many ideas can be taken from wrought iron work, as in diagrams 17 and p. 7. Bowl shapes are formed, after working the base, by lifting the level of each row of plaiting slightly above the preceding row, until the plait is lying at right angles to the base.

In a heavy log basket, this change of direction is done quickly, in the row which leaves the base to start working up the side. You may find it helpful to work round an oil drum as a guide to keeping the sides straight. The plait at the top tapers off as

7 *Plaited bowl and mat, Iris sibirica*
Shoulder bag. Rush and iris

Using plaits

8   *Miniature log basket. Gladioli*
Made by K Whitbourn

in a mat, to make the height as level as possible. The handles – 2 or 4 – are made by sewing a separate plait for each pair of handles, across the bottom and up the sides, butting the ends of the plait together underneath the basket. To take extra wear, the handles are often bound with a small plait, or twist. It will take about 50 m (60 yd) of plait 4 or 5 cm (2½ in.) wide to make a basket 40 cm (15 in.) deep and 40 cm (15 in.) across. For a lighter log basket, the sides may be worked by sewing the plait edge to edge as in the miniature in photograph 8.

Wider flat plaits are usually sewn edge to edge with a ladder stitch. The needle slips through the fold at the edge of the plait, moves over on the same level to the second plait and slides through the next fold up, before going back to the first plait in the same way. Wide strips using 8 or 9 strands can be joined together in this way for floor mats, and neatened at the ends by covering them with a narrow plait sewn on top of the edges.

A belt can be simply made from a length of plait (photograph 9), making it twice the waist size plus about 20 cm (8 in.). Fold it in half and ease the bend into a smooth flat loop while the plait is still slightly damp, and when it is dry wrap it firmly in position with a twisted strand, secured at the back. Sew the plait ends together, and fix a wooden or horn toggle on top, after checking the length of the belt for size. For the belt in the photograph, two leaves at the end of the plait were taken through the hole in the toggle, twisted into rope, one end taken through in an overhand knot, and then back through the toggle to be sewn to the plait ends.

The hair ornament to match is woven into a Josephine knot described in diagram 55 with the ends taken out to the sides and then back to the knot. The fold at the base of each iris leaf was opened out so that the silvery shine helped to lighten the colour of the plait. This was also done in the plaiting of the bowl in photograph 7 and in the coiled platter in photograph 31.

3 Woven table mats

Before making a woven basket it is as well to make one or two mats. These are quick to make and will give you the chance to practise some of the essentials of basket-making, and correct mistakes before starting on a more ambitious article. Use freshwater rushes to begin with if possible as they may be easier to use than some leaves, otherwise, choose leaves which are supple, and even in width.

ROUND MAT 15 cm (6 in.) across

Prepare 10 rushes 1·5 cm ($\frac{1}{2}$ in.) wide and a handful of thinner rushes. Cut stakes 35 cm (14 in.) long, one from the butt end of each of the 10 rushes, putting aside the other ends for weaving or plaiting.

Lay 5 stakes side by side horizontally, and as rushes taper gradually from butt to tip the work is kept even by laying a butt first at one end then at the other. This alternating of butts and tips is a general principle which is normally followed any time stakes are laid out to start working, and it is as well not to tidy the ends by cutting them straight, as the natural butts are easier to recognise quickly, and also they may be easier to thread through the lacing awl when it is time to work the border. Find the middle by folding one of the stakes in two, and place a ruler straight across the stakes, 3 cm (1$\frac{1}{2}$ in.) to the left of the centre, so as to give a clean first folding line.

Checkweave centre

Place the side of the left hand firmly on the ruler and lift stakes 2 and 4 and hold them behind the left thumb. Lay the first vertical across 1, 3 and 5, as close as possible to the ruler. Now lift up stake 1, lay down 2, lift up 3, lay down 4, pick up 5, in that order. It is most important not to drop 2 and 4 before picking up the alternating stakes as this allows the vertical stakes to drift apart, and they must be kept as close as possible. This weave is very simple, but it may not be too easy to keep it really square – if spaces are left between the stakes the shape becomes rectangular, and holes appear. Place the second vertical stake close to the first, alternating the placing of the butts as usual, and lay down stake 1, lift up 2, lay down 3, lift up 4, lay down 5. Repeat until all 5 vertical stakes are used.

Pairing

The centre is held in position and the rest of the mat worked in pairing weave, for which you need 2 weavers thinner than the stakes. Select a long strong weaver, and after pulling off the weak tip, loop it round the first stake on the left, which gives you two working ends. Take the left hand weaver in front of stake 1, behind stake 2, and lay it diagonally in front of 3. Anchor it there with your left thumb to

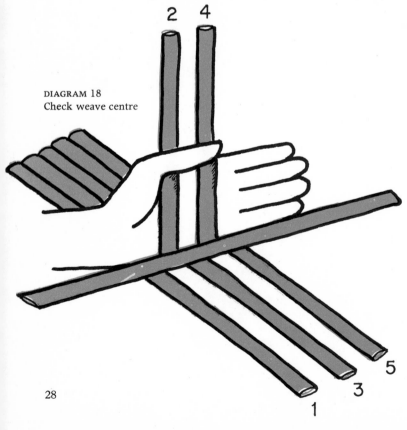

DIAGRAM 18
Check weave centre

2 4

5
3
1

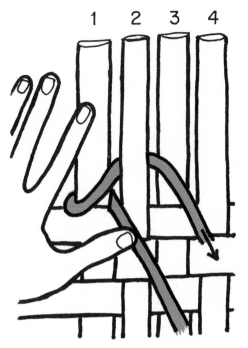

DIAGRAM 19
Pairing

stop the next movement being taken under it by mistake.

Take the new left hand weaver in front of stake 2, behind 3 and lay it diagonally in front of 4. A slight pull to the right before laying down the weaver will help to draw the stakes together. Anchor it again with the left thumb and repeat this pairing all the way round, turning the mat a quarter turn when you reach the corner, so that the working stakes are always upright, and taking extra care as you turn that the weaving sequence is not changed.

Shaping

After the first round check:

(a) that the stakes are the same length all the way round; if not, pull gently on the short end.

(b) that the centre is square; if not, holding down two stakes with the left hand, place the lacer between them, and press down the pairing to the right level.

After the second round, the stakes should be fanned out like the spokes of a wheel while continuing with the pairing so that the spaces between them become even as soon as possible.

Note: All stakes have a tendency to slope *left* so they need holding more to the right than you would expect. The central stake on opposite sides should be in a straight line.

Keep the rows of pairing as close as possible, and continue until the mat measures 15 cm (6 in.).

Joins

TIP When about 30 cm (12 in.) of the tip is left, or more if it feels too thin, lay another tip under it and use them together till the first runs out. Cut the end of the old tip so that it is hidden under the new weaver.

BUTT When the short butt has just been used, so that it is lying on the right with about 10 cm (4 in.) showing, past stake A, loop the firm tip of a new weaver round stake A, so that in each space there is now a short end and a long weaver, and slide it well down so that the loop and short ends can be completely hidden. Take a

pairing movement with both ends in the first space, then trim the end E so that it lies over – but does not overlap – stake B, and it will be hidden under the new weaver. After using the other ends together once or twice, trim the tip in the same way so that it is hidden under the long weaver. It is much more satisfactory to attend to the ends on the front of the work and hide them while damp, though it may feel a little awkward at first. The temptation to put them at the back and hope for the best only brings regrets when the (reversible) mat is turned over and the dry ends refuse to stay out of sight.

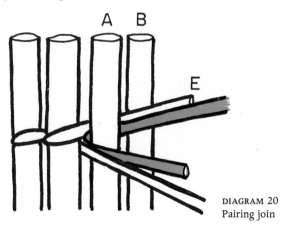

DIAGRAM 20
Pairing join

10 *Round woven mat with alternative
centre. Rush*

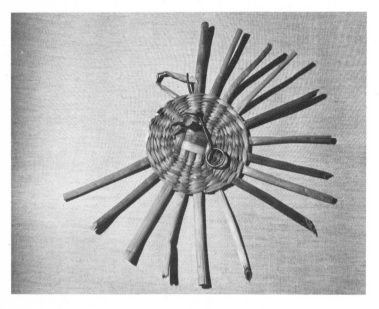

BROKEN STAKE   This is bound to happen sooner or later. Push the lacer up through several rows of weaving below the break and draw down a new length of stake over the broken end so that they overlap for 5 or 7 cm (2 in. or 3 in.). Leave the new end showing, as a reminder that the stake is not fully anchored, and trim when the work is finished.

FLAT WEAVE JOIN   If you have to join while working an area of check weave or a similar type of weave, stakes and weavers will be the same thickness, so overlap the old and new weaver for about 10 cm (4 in.) but leave a little extra showing on the left, which can be trimmed off close when the article is finished, and allows for a little unintentionally strong pulling.

Ending off a weaver before bordering
See that the depth of pairing is as even as possible all the way round, then push the lacer up through 5 cm (2 in.) of pairing in front of a stake which is just on the right of the weaver, thread the latter into the lacer and draw it down. Again, don't trim until the border is done, in case the tension needs adjusting.

Border
This is one of the simplest and most useful. Using the lacer as for ending off a weaver, draw each stake down in front of the next stake to the right, through at least 4 cm (1½ in.) of weaving. If the stake appears to be too thick to get through the eye of the lacer, cut the end diagonally, put the point into the eye and press down on the other edge of the rush as the rest of the width is pushed through. Pull each stake down firmly, at the same time moulding it round into a curve at the top with the left hand. If the 'drawing off' depth is staggered, say from 4 to 7 cm (1½ in. to 2½ in.) all the way round, it helps to prevent a ridge forming when all the ends are cut off. Before doing so, turn the mat over and check that nothing needs adjusting then pull the end of each stake as it is cut very close, so that the ends disappear completely.

Put the mat under a weight overnight, then dry it off in a current of air.

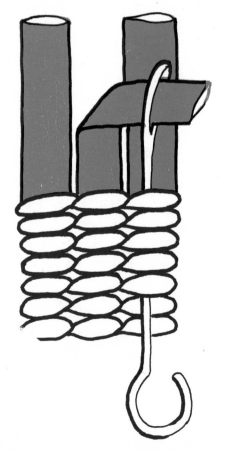

DIAGRAM 21
Drawing down stake
with lacer

Variation on the mat centre

Lay 3 stakes horizontally and 3 stakes vertically across the centre. Lift up the horizontal stakes and place another vertical stake on either side, then lift up these 2 single vertical stakes and place another horizontal stake above and below the others. Continue with pairing, as for the previous mat.

SQUARE MAT *(diagram 22)*

The centre is the same as for a round mat, but when the pairing starts the stakes are kept upright instead of being fanned out, so after two rounds, the space at the corners having increased, extra stakes are inserted. Fold a new stake into a right angle, lay it close into the corner and on the first round use the top half only, as it makes the join neater. Do this in each corner, and again after every two rounds of pairing until the mat is nearly big enough. Finish with 4 plain rounds of pairing, keeping the shape as square as possible, and before trimming the border, square up each corner against the corner of a table by tapping with the mallet.

DIAGRAM 22
Adding extra stakes
for corner

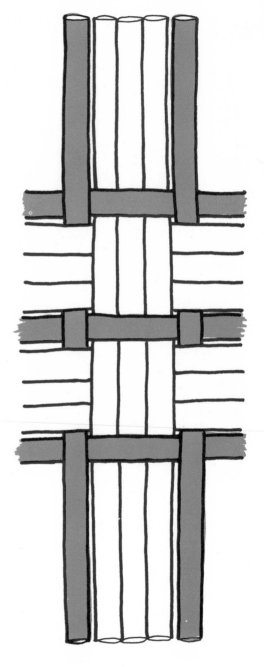

FOR AN OVAL OR OBLONG MAT

Make the centre rectangular by using
longer horizontal stakes and more vertical
stakes. It can be done in checkweave, two
or more groups of the alternative centre,
or other weaves such as twill from the
following chapter.

DIAGRAM 23
Oval centre
(alternative)

If you have to leave unfinished work for a
short time, cover it with a damp cloth to
prevent it drying out, but at the end of the
day let the air circulate round it otherwise
it may go mouldy. When it is time to do
the border, the stakes will probably have
got rather dry, so dip them in water and
cover with a damp cloth until they feel
mellow and bend easily.

4 Basic weaves

A variety of weaves can be used, either on their own or in different combinations, whether you are working a flat article or round a mould. Most of them will fall into one of the following groups:

A Those based on the check weave, in which warp and weft are usually of the same width and thickness, and equally visible.

B Those based on the pairing weave, with weft strands usually thinner than the warp, but covering the latter almost completely.

C Those which form an open weave, in which the spaces are visually as important as the working strands.

When working a flat area more than 10 cm (4 in.) wide, you will find it much easier to do if the stakes are anchored at the beginning in some way. A brick or a book will help to hold the ends in place, or they can be pinned between the table and a heavy work board, and the working ends folded back over the board.

A1 Check weave *see diagram* 18
This is a simple 'over one under one' weave, alternating, like darning, on every row. The joins are made by overlapping the old and new strands for several movements, and it is important to keep the width of the strands even. When working round a mould, arrange to have an odd number of stakes for the warp, in this way the weaving strand will automatically move over at the end of each round to alternate with the preceding row. Compare in photograph 12, the different effect when the weavers are twisted in a coil instead of lying flat.

A2 Double layer check weave
The fish in the mobile in photograph 13 are worked in a double layer check weave to give folds on two edges instead of cut ends all round. For a square, start with one strand A B folded across the middle, take half the remaining strands plus the odd

one, fold them in the same way, and slip them side by side onto A B, alternately over the top and over the bottom half until they are all used up, which gives two layers of stakes. Starting half way along each of the remaining strands, check weave across the top layer of stakes, beginning above the fold in the middle of A B. When the top layer is woven, turn the square over, and work the second layer in the same way with the other half of the weavers, after folding each one carefully in line with the fold in A B.

If the 2 finished layers are pushed outwards instead of flattened, the square can be turned into a pointed container.

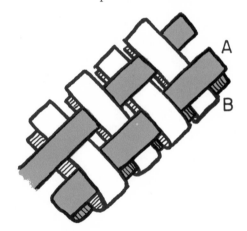

DIAGRAM 24
Double layer check weave

A3 Diagonal check weave
A flat area of check weave needs to be held together at the edges by a border of a different sort, unless each strand, at the edge, makes a double right angled fold back, as the warp and weft strands are separate. In diagonal check weave each strand, when it reaches the edge, is folded back at a right angle to become another working strand in the opposite direction. The corner strand has to take 2 right angled turns, once over and once under, so that the second half of the strand ends up alongside the first. This adapts easily to right angled shapes, whether flat, or as a double layer, or over a mould. Primitive

12 *Shoulder bag. Rush stakes, iris for coiled weavers and plaits*

13 *Mobile using iris and reed mace for fish, maize and iris for stones, pampas grass for bubbles*

DIAGRAM 25
Diagonal checkweave

DIAGRAM 26
Diagonal checkweave
doll

dolls were made like diagram 26. If you want to work a particular shape of this type, draw a pattern to size, start at one corner, and work as in diagram 25 until the next corner is reached, where the strands will change direction again. Note that in the diagram the strands reaching the bottom fold over, those at the left edge fold under. To finish off, thread the ends in to follow the weave.

This weave can be varied, like the flat plaiting of which it is an extension, by using longer strokes than a plain 'over one under one' weave. The face of the Mexican doll, photograph 14 is in diagonal check weave.

A4 Twill weave *(photograph 45)*

This is easier to keep close than a check weave. On a mould, use an odd number of stakes, weave over 2 and under 2 stakes and on every row the pattern will automatically move along, to give the diagonal twill line. (If the stroke is not too long to be practical, it can be increased to 'over 3 under 3' and for this the number of stakes round a mould must not be divisible by 3).

On the flat, every four successive rows start as follows:

Row 1: over 2, then (under 2, over 2) repeated.

Row 2: over 1, then (under 2, over 2) repeated.

Row 3: under 2, then (over 2, under 2) repeated.

Row 4: under 1, then (over 2, under 2) repeated.

DIAGRAM 27
Twill weave

B1 Pairing *see diagram* 19

As this uses 2 weavers round each stake, the result is a stronger, firmer fabric than checkweave.

B2 Brick pairing

By pairing over 2 stakes every time, and working round a mould with an odd number of stakes, the alternating stitches give a brick wall pattern. For deeper 'bricks', use an even number of stakes and pair over 2 for two rows, then slip behind an extra stake with each weaver, to alternate the bricks on the next two rows. (Photograph 23.)

B3 Block pairing

Round a mould, make the number of stakes divisible by 6. Start alternating blocks by pairing over 3 stakes singly, then over 3 stakes together. Repeat all the way round. Do the same thing for 3 or 4 rows, until the blocks look square, then on the next row exchange the position of the blocks.

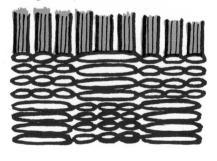

DIAGRAM 28
Block pairing

15 *Shopping basket in diagonal pairing. Square plait handle. Rush*

B4 Diagonal pairing

This is very suitable for a fairly deep round mould (photograph 15). Have the number of stakes divisible by 4, minus one. Starting with the strands in 2 successive spaces, pair over one stake and behind 3 with the first strand, then over 3 and behind one with the second strand. Repeating these 2 movements gives a short stroke followed by a long stroke, and the number of stakes will move the pattern one stake to the right on every row, giving a definite diagonal line. Check every so often that the short stroke is always immediately following the short stroke on the previous row; and as the long strokes show up well, use fairly thick weavers and discard a strand as soon as it looks too thin. An overlap join will probably be more suited to the thicker strands than a usual pairing join.

Note: if the same movements are done over stakes divisible by 4, the result will be columns of wide and narrow pairing (photograph 16). If the stakes are only divisible by 2, the result will be a pattern of long and short 'bricks'.

B5 Chain pairing

This consists of two rows of pairing, the second of which is reversed by taking the working weaver *under* the other weaver, each time, before going in front of a stake as usual (photographs 17 and 21). This gives a good line, also an interesting texture if repeated, and it has the advantage of counteracting a natural tendency to twist, if a paired article is long and narrow, such as the lid of a rectangular shopping basket.

To work an area of several rows round a mould, use 2 sets of weavers started at opposite sides of the mould, one for pairing, the other for reverse pairing. Use one set until you have nearly reached the other, then change over and use the other set. This does away with having to change the pattern at the end of each round of pairing.

To work a band of chain pairing across loose stakes, for example at intervals in a bath mat: loop 2 weavers round a stake, the top strands being in the middle, side by side. Pull back the outside strands and

16 *Basket with lid. Pairing in wide and narrow columns. Rush*

17 *Spider base lid with chain pairing down
the side and drawn up 3 plait handle. Rush*

Basic weaves

lay a second stake close to the first.
Exchange the position of the top strands
with the bottom strands, bringing the
latter on the outside first. Lay in a third
stake and repeat. This helps to hold the
stakes in position quite firmly, which is
not so easy with one round of pairing over
loose stakes.

B6 3 rod waling

(The name comes from willow basketry).
Place three weavers in successive spaces,
and work the left hand weaver in a similar
way to pairing, but going in front of 2
stakes instead of 1, each time. This gives a
bold line, either for dividing up a pattern,
or, repeated several times, for extra
strength and a close texture.

B7 Chain waling

Like chain pairing, it consists of 2 rows;
the second row of waling is reversed by
taking the left hand weaver *under* the other
2 weavers before going round a stake.

B8 4 rod waling

Place 4 weavers in successive spaces, and
work in either of the following ways:

(a) Using the left hand weaver each time,
take it in front of 2 stakes and round the
back of 2 stakes. This looks the same as 3
rod waling on both sides of the work,
which may be useful on a reversible mat,
as the back of 3 rod waling looks like
pairing.

(b) Using the left hand weaver, take it
in front of 3 stakes and round the fourth.

4 ROD WALING ROUND A CORE   As the
base of a shopping basket often gets hard
wear, a thick ridge round the edge of the
base gives extra protection to the stakes.
The core, of nearly dry, rather firm
material, is laid over the stakes (photograph
21), and each weaver, as it is laid in front
of 3 stakes, goes over the core, and when it
comes from behind the fourth stake, it
passes under the core. The ends of the core
are thinned down to overlap without extra
thickness, and the waling movement
continues past the beginning of the round,
threading underneath the core to complete
the round without a break in the pattern.

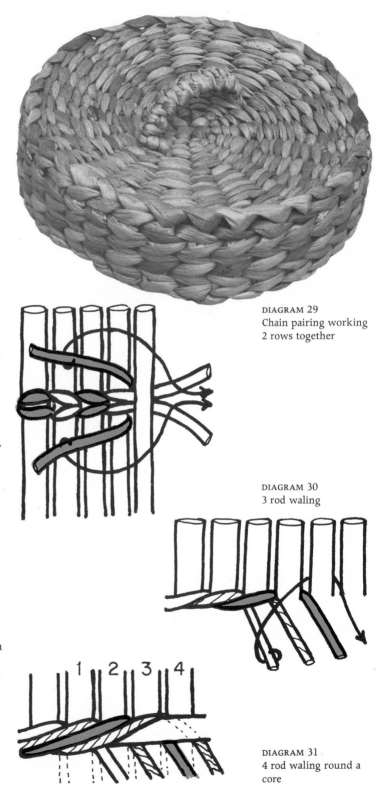

DIAGRAM 29
Chain pairing working
2 rows together

DIAGRAM 30
3 rod waling

DIAGRAM 31
4 rod waling round a
core

DIAGRAM 32
Open weave, every
third stake upright

DIAGRAM 33
Open weave moving
to the fourth place
along

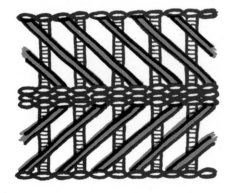

C1 Open weaves

A very light basket or mat can be made with one or more rounds of pairing holding the stakes in position at intervals. If, in the intervals between the rows, the stakes move to different positions, various open-work patterns are formed. The following are 3 of the many possibilities.

(a) With the number of stakes round a mould divisible by 3, every third stake remains vertical while the intermediate two change places. (Diagram 32.)

(b) With an even number of stakes, two neighbouring stakes change places once or several times.

(c) With the number of stakes divisible by 4, alternate stakes remain vertical, while the others move in the same direction, past 2 vertical stakes. On the next open section, the stakes move back to their original places. (Diagram 33.)

Note: remember to allow extra length on any stakes which are going to move out of the vertical line.

18   Twisted check on a round shape, ending in rope and Turk's Head. Rush

C2 Twisted check

The stakes are spaced out in pairs and the weavers work in pairs. After each making a check weave movement round 2 stakes, the weavers change places before repeating the movements round the next two stakes. At the end of the row, the stakes in each pair change places before the weaving is repeated. This pattern can be introduced as a section of openwork in a fabric, or used on its own. It will adapt usefully to a curved shape.

DIAGRAM 34
Twisted check

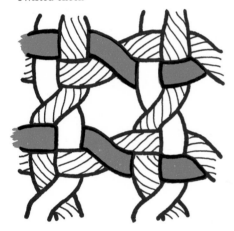

C3 3 way weaving

Working in 2 diagonal directions and a horizontal, or vertical direction, produces a very bold pattern. Lay 2 neighbouring diagonal strands across each other, the top diagonals always lying in the same direction. These top diagonals now pass under the horizontal strand while the others pass over it. Repeat from the beginning.

This pattern can be worked from one edge, or from the centre outwards.

In the lampshade in photograph 19 horizontal lines would have resulted in a lot of joins and so a rather loose fabric, whereas using vertical strands looped round the bottom rim and used double, kept all the joins at the top; it was also possible to clip them with clothes pegs to the top rim to hold them in place during the work. The plait was evolved to blend

with the main pattern as closely as possible.

For the best effect use strands as evenly matched as possible.

DIAGRAM 35
3 way weaving

39

5 Woven baskets

If a basket is to be woven from a relatively soft material, this has to be taken into account when planning its shape. A wide based basket carrying any weight would soon loose its shape, so shopping baskets are usually rectangular with a narrow base, or bucket shaped. If the handles are part of a strong plaited circle, going down the sides and under the basket, they will take the weight of the contents very efficiently, so the basket could have a slightly wider base. If, however, the basket is only meant to carry a light weight, such as bread rolls, or is to be used in one position, as a container for flowers, for instance, the restrictions on the shape apply far less.

MOULDS

Again, because of the soft material, it is helpful to work over a mould which will keep the shape in position during the making and until the article has dried off.

Wooden moulds are good, if they are smooth and exact, as the work grips the wood, and tacks can be inserted in the corners to stop the base moving out of place. If the mould is roughly made, however, any little projections may obstruct the removal of the finished article, and damage it. For the same reason, if a tin is used, it should not have a projecting rim round the base. Flower pots are useful – a large one will serve as a mould for a bucket bag; and shallow cooking dishes are often good shapes for flower containers. Some strips of adhesive cloth across the base of glass or plastic moulds will help to prevent the base slipping on the smooth surface.

Sometimes, making a basket for a particular purpose may mean having to improvise a mould, if wood is not available. If something soft, such as a cereal packet, happens to be the right size, pad it firmly with magazines to keep its shape during the work and put it in a plastic bag so that the cardboard doesn't soften in contact

with the damp work. An article can always be covered, but if its shape gets smaller as the work progresses, it will not be removable.

STAKES

The time spent selecting stakes is never wasted. Choose a size suitable for the size of article you plan to make – in a small basket, big thick stakes can look clumsy, while very thin stakes in a shopping basket would not wear well. Have them as evenly matched as possible, for the sake of both strength and appearance. The base of leaves and rushes is the strongest part, so start measuring the stakes from that end.

Number of stakes needed

We will suppose that your strands are 1 cm ($\frac{1}{2}$ in.) wide. Measure all round the top of your mould, and that number of centimetres divided by 2, (that number of inches) gives the number of stakes that you need. This is because each stake goes up the side of the mould twice, as well as across the base. If the stakes are wider than 1 cm ($\frac{1}{2}$ in.), less will be needed, but if they are smaller, use enough to have them nearly touching all the way round, to make a firm basket.

Length of stakes needed

Add together the following measurements:
Once across the base.
Twice up the side (of the basket).
Twice the border allowance of at least 10 cm (4 in.), depending on the type of border and the thickness of the stakes.

This gives the length of each stake, and for a round or square shape, they will all be the same. For a rectangular shape, there will be two different lengths. The width of the base, in cm or half inches, will give the number of longer stakes, while the length of the base gives the number of shorter stakes. For example, to make a basket 20 cm (8 in.) long by 11 cm (4½ in.) wide by 9 cm (3½ in.) high, you will need 20 stakes measuring $11+(9 \times 2)+(10 \times 2)=$ 49 cm (19½ in.) and 11 stakes measuring $20+18+20=58$ cm (23 in.).

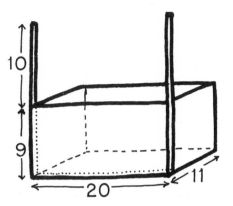

DIAGRAM 36
Measuring stakes for a basket

BASES

Square and rectangular bases

These are the easiest shapes to start with, as the base can be completely covered with check or twill weave, like the centre of a mat, and the stakes, as they reach the edge of the base, will be lying close together ready to go up the sides of the mould.

To start a rectangular base: turn the mould upside down, mark the centre of the base, and lay the long stakes in position alternating butts and tips and covering the base completely, with the middle of each stake over the middle of the base. Tie them firmly to the mould with a soft string across the centre, and using the shorter stakes, work in check or twill weave from the string to the right hand edge. Put a temporary tack in the corners to stop the last stake from moving out of place, turn the mould round and work the second half of the base in the same way, when the base is completely covered, tie it on, if the corners are not tacked (photograph 20). Loop a strong fine weaver round a corner stake on the left of a short side and pair very carefully along the edge of the mould, as this sets the shape of the basket, then lay the mould on its side and continue working in close rounds, using any of the weaves described in the previous chapter, which suit the style and purpose of the basket. Finish off with the mat border, or one of those described later in this chapter. Leave the basket under a weight over-night, or roll it well, then let it dry and remove the mould.

General notes

It is neater to start working up the sides of a basket from the corner stake on the left of a *short* side, as any irregularities due to pattern changes will be less noticeable there.

If an odd number of stakes is needed for the weaving of the sides of the basket, start by laying the thick butt of a weaver up the first corner of the mould to make an extra stake, and use the other end as one of the two weavers needed for pairing.

Keep the thickness of the weavers well balanced, if necessary cutting off a too thick butt, or overlapping tips to keep the thickness even.

Stakes always tend to lean to the left, so counteract this by holding them slightly to the right.

Measure the height of the work at intervals and keep it level by pressing down with the lacer where necessary, and particularly at the top before bordering. Guide lines may be drawn across a wooden mould and can be most helpful.

Roll the work while still damp, or tap with a mallet. If the mould is round, roll the basket itself against a smooth surface.

When starting to work on the basket again after an interval, as you prepare the weavers, redamp the unworked portion only, of the basket. It serves no useful purpose to damp the rest, there will be difficulty drying it out and it may spot with mould. A damp towel wrapped completely round the stakes will mellow them.

The base of an oblong mould may be worked in pairing for extra strength, but allow for the 'take up' in the pairing by adding to the length of the long stakes (photograph 21).

20 *Starting a rectangular basket*

21 *Paired base of basket with edge of 4 rod
wale over a core*

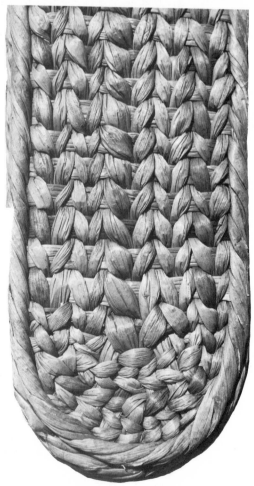

Round bases

(A) CHECK WEAVE To work a round area
in check or twill weave, it is easier to work
a square which just covers the circular
base, then carefully undo the corners until
the stakes can be laid closely over the edge
and up the side of the mould, holding
them in place with the first round of
pairing. Tie the base on before undoing
the corners.

(B) CHECK AND PAIRING WEAVES To
make a base like a mat with a check centre
and the stakes fanned out during the
pairing, would leave the stakes too far
apart at the edge of the base. This can be
remedied by working a double centre,
either by laying one check centre on top
of another, or by using each stake double,
while making the same size of centre. In
both cases the first round of pairing must
be very closely and firmly done, round the
double stakes; after the second round,
open out the corner stakes and use them
singly. Do the same with the neighbouring
stakes in the following rounds, working a
plain round in between if possible, but the
stakes must all be singled by the last round
which fits the base. Tie the work onto the
mould so that the weavers are pointing to
the right, ready to continue weaving.

(C) SPIDER BASE Cut 7
stakes the right length, place all butts
together, and tie the stakes together very
tightly in the middle. A constrictor knot
remains tight when the ends have been
firmly pulled (diagram 37). Each strand
must now be folded back on itself like a
hairpin, and fanned out in a circle of alternating butts and tips. Loop a strong fine
weaver round one of the lower stakes in
the flower-like centre, and pair round
closely, seeing that the lower stakes are
drawn up to the same level as the others.
Continue pairing for 5 cm (2 in.) then with
the lacer draw half stakes down through
the pairing beside alternate stakes. After
4 cm (2 in.) of pairing add more stakes in
the same way, so that by the time the work
is the size of the base, the stakes are close
enough to make a firm basket (photograph
17).

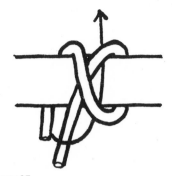

DIAGRAM 37
Constrictor knot

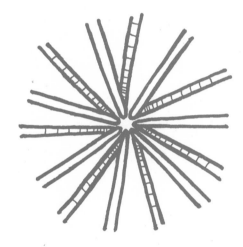

DIAGRAM 38
Spider base

LIDS

To work a lid for a straight sided basket
Before taking the basket off the mould,
turn it upside down and work a base to
fit over the base of the basket and then
pair round the side for about 3 or 4 cm
(1½ or 2 in.). After bordering and drying
off, remove the lid and it can hardly fail to
fit when put in its right place.

BORDERS

The type of border you choose will depend
on the kind of wear that it can expect.

Border 1
Shown in diagram 21, this would be a
practical one for any basket, though others
may be quicker to do and others again are
more decorative. The following are a selection of different types, which you can
develop or adapt, remembering that for
hard wear the ends of the border are best
hidden within the weaving, and the border
itself should be close and firm.

Border 2
As for border 1, but thread each stake
down in front of the second stake along,
not the first. This gives a rope-like edge,
and if it is preceded by a row of 3 rod
waling, the edge will look like a close plait,
as in the basket in photograph 15.

Border 3, trac
This is a weaving sequence, worked with
each stake in turn. Taking stake no. 1,
behind no. 2 and in front of no. 3 before
drawing down, as in the square mat in
photograph 11 is a simple trac, but the last
stakes must always be threaded through
the first stakes to complete the pattern
before drawing down.
   The hat border (photograph 22) is a
much longer trac, with the stakes kept as
flat as possible. Each stake was taken in
front of one stake, behind 2 stakes, in
front of one stake, behind 2 stakes, in front
of one stake, and behind one. Diagram 39
shows a simple trac: in front of 2, behind
1, in front and behind one.

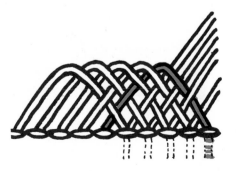

DIAGRAM 39
Trac border

43

Border 4, simple fold

This and the following border are easy to do, as they need no threading down. 4 or 5 rows before the weaving ends, fold each stake over so that the fold will eventually extend 3 cm (1¼ in.) beyond the edge of the weaving; complete the last 4 or 5 rows round the folded stakes. Trim the ends close. This would be suitable for a table mat or bath mat.

Border 5, close fold

This border hardly shows at all. Work as for the previous border, but thread one of the weavers through all the folded stakes, and then pull each stake down level with the edge of the weaving.

DIAGRAM 40
Folded border

Border 6, stiffened

For a wastepaper basket which is usually picked up by the border, the stiffening helps the basket to keep its shape. Take each stake behind the next one and out to the front, threading the last one through the first loop. Lay a circle of cane over the stakes just below the edge, after paring the ends of the cane so that where they overlap the thickness of the ring remains the same. Pick up each stake in turn, wrap it round the cane, and thread down in front of the next stake along.

Border 7

Quick border for decorating small baskets. On the last round of pairing, every time a weaver goes in front of one stake and behind the next, the first of these two stakes is turned back and bent down behind the weaver and the second stake and taken out to the front, diagonally. This makes a series of little angled folds along the top. The ends are trimmed at an angle, fairly close to the pairing, so that they in turn form a series of points.

Border 8, plait

This is worked in 3 rounds:

   (a) Fold each stake behind the next on the right, and out to the front diagonally, lying flat against the basket. Thread the last one through the first loop.

   (b) Fold each stake up and under the next on the right at a corresponding angle. Watch the width of the plait as you make it, to be sure that it stays even, as it has a tendency to rise off the top. Keep it pressed flat on the basket.

   (c) Fold each stake down and thread behind the next stake, through the plait and several rows of the weaving below. This forms the top edge of the plait, and as it is pulled down by the lacer, shape it into position. Trim closely.

Note. It is easier to draw off a border through waling, or pairing round 2 or more stakes, than through pairing round single stakes.

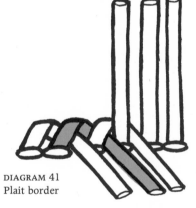

DIAGRAM 41
Plait border

DIAGRAM 42
Plait border

DIAGRAM 43
Plait border

FRAME BASKETS

If you want a basket to be quite rigid this can be achieved by working the soft material round a frame of cane, willow, hazel or other pliable rods. The result will be strong and light. Making the frame needs care and practice, but it is worth the effort.

The melon basket (photograph 24) was started with two hoops of cane about 25 cm (10 in.) across, and half of one was covered for the handle. The rim hoop was placed inside the handle hoop, and where they touch they were lashed together. This is done with a strong rush working anti-clockwise closely round the junction, wrapping round each cane in turn and forming a series of overlapping squares. Work each one to 5 or 7 cm (2 or 3 in.) across, and this will give room to spring in the two main ribs from end to end, one on either side, and slightly longer than half a hoop, so that the basket has a base to sit on, otherwise it will rock (photograph 25). Start weaving closely round the square from rim to rim for about 4 cm (1½ in.), at both ends of the handle. This will give room for more ribs to be inserted, 3 on each side, and the weaving continues round them all, first at one end then at the other,

in order to keep the shape balanced, and packing the rows closely together. If however the weaving builds up in the middle, turn round a rib and go back to the edge to straighten the line. The weaving should end in the middle of the basket.

The frame of the rectangular flower basket (photograph 26), made of pussy willow, started with the double handle rods being bound into the top rim. The struts of willow and very thick rushes were bent at the ends and wrapped into place and then the weaving was worked from either end. It incorporated wrapping round the struts, to cover them. The box in photograph 27 is a different type of work on a frame and can be seen at the British Museum.

26   Rectangular frame basket. Pussy willow and rush

HANDLES

There are two methods of providing a basket with a handle: one is to insert the strands for making the handle, into the basket, work a suitable plait the necessary length for the handle, and thread the ends back into the basket (photographs 15 and 17); the other is to make an independent length of plait, and apply it to the basket (photographs 8, 12, 16). Which ever method is used, choose strong strands without cracks or flaws, as the wear on a handle is considerable. There is no reason why another type of material should not be used, as long as it blends in with the rest of the work. Leather should wear well, and it looks good with rush, and the basket in photograph 27a has some waling and all the plaiting worked in soft shades of fillis string. The plaiting also protects the corners, another area of hard wear.

(a) Inserting handles

Break off the weak tips of the strands and insert them under the border and 2 cm (1 in.) of weaving, pulling them through half way. If the handle is to be a thick one the strands can be divided between 2 neighbouring spaces, and should be long enough to complete the handle without a join, if possible. (About 120 cm for a shopping basket.) Gather them up into 2 equal groups, if making a rope handle, or 3 or more for a plait, then work the necessary length, separate the strands into 2 (or 4) groups again, place them on either side of the border, and draw them through the same hole (or 2 holes) to correspond with the start of the handle. Thread the ends away making sure that some of the strongest ends follow some of the weaving for several movements.

   In a rectangular shopping basket, the handles should span the middle third of the long sides.

   In a small basket, with the handle crossing the middle, a length equal to about half the circumference of the basket usually looks right.

27   Ancient Egyptian cosmetic box. Papyrus rind. The British Museum, London

47

(b) Handles made from a continuous plait

The length of the plait has to cover four times the height of the basket and twice the width of the base as well as the length of the two handles. The ends are joined under the basket, and a splice would be the neatest way of joining a flat plait (see page 17) – otherwise bind the ends firmly, butt them together after trimming, and sew into place.

The handle plait can be incorporated in the weaving of the basket if it is placed in position as soon as the base is completed (photograph 16). In this way the weaving can be worked round both the plait and the stakes behind it. If the plait is applied after the rest of the basket is completed, it can either be sewn into place as invisibly as possible with soft strong string, or else held in place by short lengths of thin plaiting or rope, worked from a stake on the left of the handle to a stake on the right of the handle, at regular intervals up the side of the basket.

The handles themselves may be reinforced, as in a log basket, by binding with twisted strands or a fine plait.

6 Seating

Chair seating with rushes, reedmace or long iris leaves is practical – the result is hard wearing, comfortable and attractive in appearance, with the soft mixed colours of green gradually changing over the years to fawn and brown. It is a method of seating which has been continuously in use in Britain since the fourteenth century, Oxfordshire being one of the main centres of the work, but the best rushes for seating were the salt water rushes imported from Holland – shorter than the freshwater rushes but very supple, tough, and a beautiful golden colour. Unfortunately there are few of these now available. In order to prevent the periodic flooding which has been so disastrous at times, Holland has been gradually enclosing her salt water lakes with dykes and dams, with the result that the rushes are disappearing as the salt water becomes fresh. However other rushes of medium thickness and leaves of some reasonable length will make very good seating materials. For a small chair a length of at least 1 m (1 yd) would be needed, and the longer the material, the easier the work will be.

The seats will have the corners raised above the general level of the rails, so that they hold the first rounds of the work in the correct position. It is easier to practise on a square or rectangular shape to begin with.

The cord itself is made up of several strands which, when smoothly twisted together, look like one round firm cord and not like one strand wrapped round another. The movement is a continuous pulling-twisting-stroking one done with one hand, while the other follows along holding the twist and helping to smooth out any unevenness.

The direction of the twist in traditional English seating is *away* from the nearest corner, and no twisting is done on the underside of the seat, as this helps to hold in the padding. Continental methods may differ. The size of the coil depends on the type of chair – old fashioned chairs were often done in a fine twist of about 3 to the cm (7 to the in.) whereas modern chairs might have cords of nearly 1 cm ($\frac{1}{3}$ in.) each. Whatever size has been decided on, one of the main objects is to keep it as even as possible. After working for a while, your fingers will become more aware of the size and smoothness of the cord produced, but it is harder, and takes longer, to work a fine, even cord than a thick one.

There are several different ways of working, and when undoing an old chair seat it is always interesting to note what method was used.

To start
Mellow the material and prepare it by breaking off any weak tips and, if using rushes, expel the air by pulling them firmly between thumb and forefinger towards the tip. Start with two or more butts tied together by a reef knot, place it at the left hand end of the back rail with some of the rushes over, and some under it so that the cord can be held firmly over the front rail by the left hand corner. *Twist away from the corner, pull tightly and lay over the rail

DIAGRAM 44
Reef knot

49

close to the left corner, continuing the twist down the side of the rail as well. Bring it up through the middle of the frame, and reversing the twist so that it is still *away* from the corner, lay it over the left hand rail. Bring the cord up through the middle of the frame, move the chair round a quarter turn clockwise so that the right hand corner now becomes the working corner, close at hand, and repeat from *. A right angle must be carefully formed each time, so when the cord goes to the left it is placed rather than pulled. If it is pulled too hard and the angle gets distorted, the chair seat will end up with a hole in the middle. When you meet the original reef knot at the end of the first round, cut the cord just inside the frame so that the knot drops off. Contrary to most peoples apprehensive expectation this will not cause the rest of the work to fall apart.

Joins

As soon as the cord begins to feel thin, join in another rush or leaf.
(1) *A reef knot* is strong, but it is slow and several of them become bulky.
(2) *A half hitch* is quick and convenient but it can't be used if the whole cord needs renewing.

Place these joins anywhere between the worked sections of the corners, in this way they will eventually be hidden as the work continues. Try not to have them too close to each other, or to the corners.
(3) *Laying in a new butt* in the corner, leaving several cm on the underside. As the cord comes up the centre, new and old strands are twisted together, and the short end underneath can be tucked in or cut, later on. A very useful join.

When nearing the centre and the work is closing up, a butt can be pinched between the underside of the seat and the cord to be thickened, before it crosses the centre. This will be enough to hold it until properly gripped by the twist going over the rail.

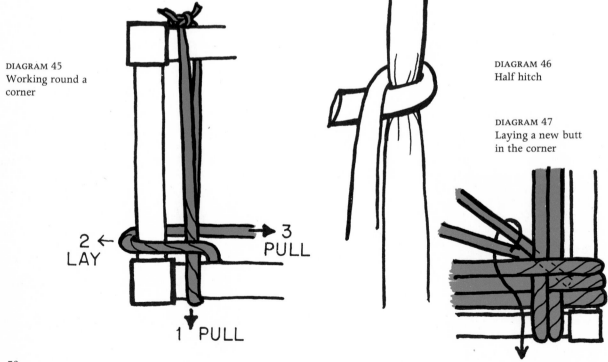

DIAGRAM 45
Working round a corner

2 ← LAY

3 → PULL

1 ↓ PULL

DIAGRAM 46
Half hitch

DIAGRAM 47
Laying a new butt in the corner

Rectangular shape

Keeping the cords firm, even and lying very close to each other, continue until the shorter rails are nearly filled in. When one rail will only take 2 or 3 more coils, instead of continuing to the opposite rail, wrap the coil 2 or 3 times round the first rail to fill it up before continuing to the other side and wrapping in the same way there. This allows a little more space for the fingers when working the centre, and also gives the coils room to settle there. Fill the remaining portion of the longer rails with a figure of eight movement of the coil going from one rail, up the centre and over the opposite rail, etc. Remember that the coil builds up twice as quickly at the centre as on the rails, so keep the coil fairly flat and well pressed back in the centre.

Use the lacer to help thread the last coils through the centre, and when the seat is complete, take the last coil round a strand coming from the opposite rail on the underside, form an overhand knot in the middle and tuck the ends in.

DIAGRAM 48
Working the figure of eight

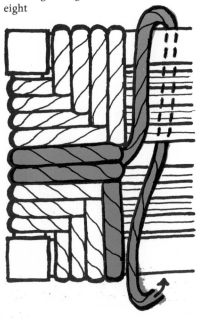

Padding

This can be done as the work progresses, but the underside of the seat will be flatter if it is left till the seat is finished. After a few hours, turn it upside down, take some dry but still pliable pieces of rush and with the aid of the packing stick push them in about half way along one side and press firmly into the corner, gradually working back towards the centre and turning the chair round to attend to the corresponding corner in the same way. When all the seat feels firm, roll the top with a small length of dowelling, towards the diagonal lines, this will help to smooth and polish it. The padding improves the look of the seat and also helps to prevent wear against the rails. If the cords have been carefully placed at the corners, the diagonal lines will be absolutely straight. Allow the chair to air well before covering it with a cushion as otherwise it may go mouldy.

Shaped seat

If the seat is neither square nor rectangular the extra space on the front rail is filled in early on in the working of the seat so as to bring it back to a rectangular shape. This can be done in several ways.

METHOD (A)   Tie a bundle of 20 or 30 rushes together tightly, half by the butts and half by the tips and then tie the string to the left hand rail or the left side of the back rail, pick up enough rushes from the bundle to make a cord, work round the front two corners and tie temporarily to the right hand rail. Go back to the bunch and repeat, as many times as will be needed to make the unworked space on the front rail equal to the back rail, and then the work can continue right round and proceed as for a rectangular seat.

METHOD (B)   The following method usually gives a better finish: work one complete round, and after passing the back left hand corner, divide the cord into two sections, leave one half aside, add fresh material to the other half to bring it up to size, and work round the two front corners. With a clothes peg, clip the cord to the one already beside the right hand rail, and go back to the half cord left behind.

DIAGRAM 49
Packing stick

Join on whatever is necessary to bring it up to size and work round the two front corners again. When the pegged cord end is reached, use the best of it to add to the working cord and continue round the back corners. This means that 2 cords are worked round the front two corners every time one cord is worked round the back corners and this is repeated until the unworked portions of the front and back rails are the same length, then the work continues as for a square or rectangular seat.

Square variation
A double cord effect is produced by working a figure of eight between opposite rails before completing the left hand side of each corner. This means that the cord will go over the rails in the following order: B, A, C, A, C, B, D, B, etc. (photograph 28).

Continental variation
In this pattern, the cords at either end of the front rail, instead of increasing in size gradually, do so in long steps, giving quite a different shape to the seat. Start at the right-hand corner, and keep the twist going in the same direction all the time, unlike the traditional English method. Go over the rails in the following order: right, front, right, across to left, front, left, then (right, left) 3 times, and repeat from the beginning. When only 2 more cords will be needed at each side to fill in the extra space on the front rail, make the 'steps' shorter by taking fewer turns between the right and left rails. Then continue as for a normal rectangular seat. A further variation consists of changing the figure of eight in the long 'steps' to a complete wrap around the frame. This keeps the cords at a higher level near the front of the chair, so that there is less wear produced by pressure on the front rail.

28   Square seat variation. Rush

D

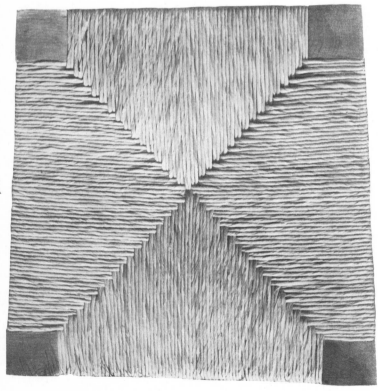

A   C

B

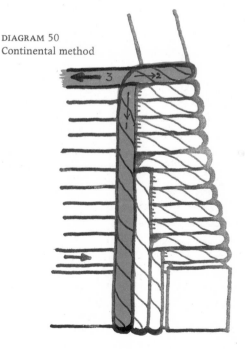

DIAGRAM 50
Continental method

Repairs
Sometimes a chair has one or two broken
strands which can be replaced by threading
a new cord through and knotting it underneath to one of the other strands. If the
centre is worn it can be undone and re-
worked as a complete section, but if other
portions are worn it is unlikely to be worth
repairing, there would be so much to
take out.

Chair back
The back of a chair can be done to match
the seat, as in the smaller of the two black
chairs. It has had the top section of the
back, with one rail, removed, and enough
of the side rails between the 'corners'
planed down to accommodate the width
of the cord (photograph 29).
    The childs chair in photograph 30 has
the distinctive Orkney back. The thick coil
of straw or rush is held in place by stitches
of string (see diagram 51) and as it curves
back in a U shape at the sides, a stitch goes
through the loop of the U and into a hole
drilled into the frame of the chair, before
starting on the next row. The top coil is
wrapped in between the linking stitches.

7 Coiled work

A twisted coil similar to that which is used for seating can be worked up in quite a different way. By stitching it together with string, rushes, or supple leaves, mats and basket shapes can be built up. Any of the usual leaves or rushes may be used in the coil, including shorter leaves, as they are gathered together, twisted and held by the stitching, or if the coil is to be completely covered it can be a length of cane. Generally it will be found that material which is thin in relation to the size of the coil is most suitable, as the continuous insertion of new strands is hidden within the thickness of the coil, and hardly noticeable. A funnel is a useful tool because it acts as a gauge as well as making the work easier to handle. Old fashioned bee skeps made of coiled straw were often made by using a horn in the same way. Use a size of funnel that allows your coil to pass through comfortably, so that if it gets too tight or too loose you will quickly notice (photograph 31).

String sewn coil

Threading your needle with a long length of soft strong string such as fillis and holding the coil in the left hand, start wrapping it tightly with the string, about 4 cm (1½ in.) from the end, working towards the tapered point. Push the end of the coil round into a tight little circle which you will be stitching from right to left and sew right through to the centre, round both coils a few times, to keep the centre firm. Now start stitching, over the top coil from front to back, through the top of the coil below, and out to the front. The needle is inserted on the right of a stitch at the back and comes out at the front just on the left. At first the stitches will be very close, but they will soon start to separate as they curve outwards, and should be kept evenly spaced. When the stitches get too far apart, start new lines of stitches at regular intervals. As the string runs out knot in a new end as for plaiting (diagram 13). On the

DIAGRAM 51
Coil, using funnel

31   Coiled platter. Crocosmia

last round, thin out the coil and taper it so that it can be threaded into the coil below, and if you like you can sew back over the last row to make V shaped stitches round the edge.

Covered coil

There are many different stitches which can be used to cover a coil, and some superb examples can be seen in American Indian basketry. The base being the strongest part of each leaf or rush used in the stitching, is threaded through the needle, and a new tip is laid along the coil so that it will be bound in and ready for use when needed. The old end will then be laid against the coil and bound in during the work.

The following are some of the basic stitches:

FIGURE OF EIGHT STITCH   After coiling the centre tightly as before, the stitch goes *over the top coil and through to the front, under the coil below and through to the back, out to the front between the two coils, to start again at *. This method is slow but strong.

FOR AN OVAL SHAPE: hold the core in the left hand and bend about 15 cm (6 in.) of the end down into a U, and hold it close to the main length. Wrap the bent end and then come up between the coils and start the figure of eight stitch by going over the top coil as before. When you reach the end of the short section, wrap the coil on the bend and hold it in very closely as you start off on the straight side again with the usual stitch. On the last round you may need to go over the single coil again if there are gaps to be filled.

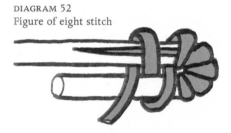

DIAGRAM 52
Figure of eight stitch

LAZY SQUAW   A short stitch wraps round the top coil once from front to back, then a long stitch wraps over the top coil again and comes out below (or through) the lower coil. The long stitch is the slow one to do, so the lazier the squaw, the more short stitches there are between each long stitch. How to work a rectangular shape is shown in the mat in photograph 32.

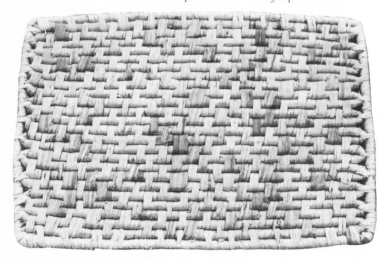

32   Imported mat in lazy squaw stitch

DIAGRAM 53
Lazy squaw stitch

33 *Imported linen basket in mariposa*
stitch
34 *Triangular shaping of basket lid*

MARIPOSA   This stitch forms a kind of
knot between the coils. Try an oval shape
to begin with, so as to get used to the stitch
before having to adjust the wraps to fit a
curve.

Fold the end of the coil down into a U
as before, and hold the long and short ends
in the left hand. This time as you wrap
round the bend, wrap forward and over
the top, then down through the centre.
When the bend is covered wrap the 2 coils
together once or twice before starting the
stitch: *come up between the coils, on the
left of the last stitch, cross over it to the
right and go in between the coils, wrap up
and over the top coil, towards the left,
wrap it again, continue the wrap straight
down and go in below the lower coil.
Repeat from *. On the bend, as in a circle,
more than one stitch will be taken down
into the same space to increase the number
of spaces on the following row. Photographs 33 and 34.

The mariposa weave can be expanded to
give a more open effect by wrapping the
top coil 4 times between the knots, holding
the top coil at a set distance from the lower,
and after going in below the lower coil,
wrapping the linking stitch 2 or 3 times
to keep the coils apart.

The figure of eight and the mariposa
stitches can be used to give blocks of
different textures in the same basket.
Separate the sections with a long stitch
over 2 coils.

To make baskets of these stitches you
need care in shaping, and a good eye, as
there is nothing else to help the sides to
flow smoothly and evenly.

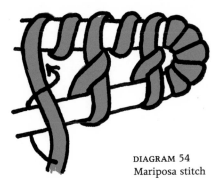

DIAGRAM 54
Mariposa stitch

8 Knotting

Because leaves and rushes can be worked
into a coil, rope or plait, these in turn can
be used for knotting in many different
ways. Tools are not essential, but the
following will be found useful:

For small knots: a large tapestry needle for
pulling strands through. A doubled piece
of stiff wire can be used for thicker
stuff.

For big knots: a fid, which is a thick metal
bodkin, or a meat skewer will make a
space for threading the working ends,
and a swedish fid with a groove allows
the end to be fed through while keeping
the space open.

For shaping flat knots: a sheet of cork or
strawboard and strong pins will help to
hold the loops in position.

Use good quality materials, without
cracks or weaknesses, and if a strand is
made up of several leaves, give a twist to
each movement so that they form a smooth,
firm coil.

The following are just a few of the
different types of knots, and ideas for
using them. The full range, with endless
possibilities, is to be found in *Ashley's
Book of Knots.*

FLAT OR MAT KNOTS

These two dimensional knots can be used
for floor mats, table mats, key guards,
jewellery, etc – the scale may differ but
the principle of making them is the same.
If the mats are made up of several parallel
cords, it will probably be necessary to sew
them together at intervals to stop them
moving out of place in use.

(a) The Josephine knot, or Carrick bend
This is a simple and beautiful knot which
can be repeated or developed into a variety
of different shapes. To work it, take a
length of plait and pin it to the board in the
middle, to give 2 working ends. Make a
loop with the end on the left, and pin it
where it crosses. Lay the right hand strand
under the loop and weave the end round
in an 'over one, under one' weave as in the
diagram.

Starting successive knots from alternate
sides, a length of spaced out Josephine
knots makes a handsome belt. The strands
can be used double or treble for a bolder
effect. And for a variation, try working 2
knots almost touching, and then a space
before repeating them.

DIAGRAM 55
Josephine knot

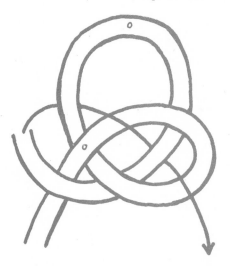

DIAGRAM 56
Josephine knot

A succession of knots can be worked into a curve by making the strand on one side much shorter than the other, between knots. They can then be joined up to make a circular or oval mat after an even number of knots, and the ends followed through to double the strands in the original knot.

The hair ornament in photograph 9 is a Josephine knot with the ends taken further away and then back to the loop they have just left.

(b) The prolong knot

Often used to make stair treads on ships, it can be made in different lengths. Start by making a Josephine knot in the middle of a long strand. Pin it at the top, and lengthen the 2 loops so that it looks as if you are working with 6 strands altogether. Work a portion of 6 plait (see pages 16–17) and every time the ends are threaded out at the corners the knot can be considered complete, and threading one end back to lie beside the other forms the loop to correspond with the top loop. It can be continued to double the cord all the way round, and finish off with the ends away from the edge and sew them down.

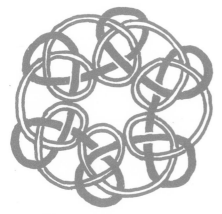

DIAGRAM 57
Mat of Josephine
knots

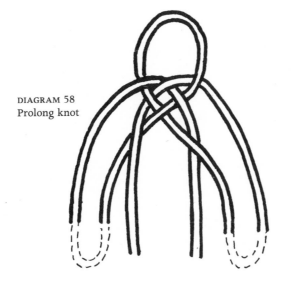

DIAGRAM 58
Prolong knot

DIAGRAM 59
Prolong knot
completed

59

(c) The Turk's head (single line)
This is usually a tubular knot but it can also be worked and used, flattened out. A very simple one, starting as (a) above, with a Josephine knot, is completed by bringing the ends past each other to form the fourth loop, and then continuing alongside to double or treble the cord. This is how the flat key guard (photograph 35) was worked, the ends being finally brought up and over the keyring and held in place by 2 whippings.

The table mat (photograph 36) is another turk's head, with 5 loops instead of 4.

35   Key ring tags, Turk's Head and knob knot; Turk's Head beads; purse in 3 rod waling and chain pairing made from day lily

Holding the working end in the right hand, loop it from right to left and back to the right again as in diagram 6. Pin it to the board where it crosses at the top and with the working end, weave round the pin in an 'over one, under one' movement, starting by going over, at (a). The ends join up as before and can parallel the original line 2 or 3 times. If the knot is eased out at the centre so that it will fit round a cylinder, it can be made into a ring shape, or tightened up into a gathering hoop or covering round another article. The tightening up has to be done gradually, taking up the slack loop by loop with a blunt bodkin, right through the knot. An impatient pull on one end will just distort the knot. Worked very firmly round a knitting needle it will make a bead.

DIAGRAM 60
4 bight (or loop)
Turk's Head

DIAGRAM 61
5 bight Turk's Head

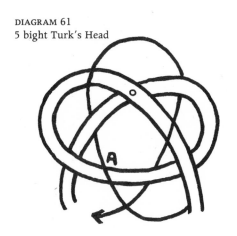

DIAGRAM 62
Standing Turk's Head

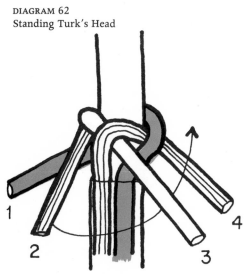

(d) The Standing Turk's head

May look the same, but it is worked differently. It can be tied with any number of ends, round a core, and it can be done with much shorter leaves for that reason, so the beads in photograph 35 are made of the white inner sweetcorn leaves. To make beads on a knitting needle or dowelling, use supple leaves which will twist into a smooth coil, space them round the core and tie in the middle very tightly with a constrictor knot (diagram 37). Both ends of the same leaf are brought together and twisted at right angles to the core, just before using. The beads in photographs 35 and 37 are made with 4 strands or groups of leaves, but the same movements are repeated round the core until the last strand is reached, whatever the number. With 4 strands, number them from 1 to 4 and lay 1 over 2, 2 over 3, 3 over 4 and 4 over 1; as 1 is already bent down, this means that you thread 4 through the first loop. Even out the size of the loops, to make the shape clear. Number the ends again, starting anywhere, and working round in the same direction, lay 1 *under* 2 and up, out of the way, 2 under 3 in the same way, 3 under 4, and 4 under 1. Check that 4 is going through the correct

DIAGRAM 63
Standing Turk's Head

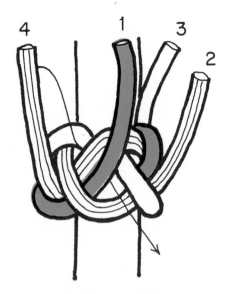

comes out at one end of the knot. When it is dry and taken off the core the ends are trimmed very close – add a touch of glue if there is to be any friction. The knot will have been worked snug, one loop at a time, while still slightly damp.

In the pendant in photograph 35 the two colours are produced by using 2 sweet corn strands and 2 iris strands. The circles are made of one length of round plait (diagram 6), coiled 3 times round the bead and once to make the hanging loop. The variation in colour is the natural change in the leaves. The bell pull (photograph 38) is started with a length of rope worked in the middle of the leaves, so that the ends can form part of the tassel. After looping it and tying tightly under the rope, insert 2

37   Beads made from day lily

loop by pulling to make sure it leads to 1. These two rounds form the basic knot, and the rest consists of doubling or trebling the strands. Each end will be lying beside a loop, and make sure that they are all lying on the same side of their respective loops. Starting with any end, *thread it through twice, parallel to its neighbouring loop, and it will come out in the same space as another end. Pick up the new end, and repeat from *. When all 4 ends have been used, they should be evenly spaced out and all the loops double. This can be repeated once or twice more according to the size of the knot, but the very last threading, instead of coming out in the middle of the knot, is taken right into the centre of the knot against the core and

bunches, at right angles to each other and to the core, giving 4 working groups, and tie again tightly immediately below. Turn the core so that the loop is underneath before starting to work the knot, in this way the working ends will join the rope ends to form the tassel when the knot is complete. The same idea could be used to make a brush, using suitably tough grasses or leaves.

(e) A Button, or Knob knot

The manrope knot is similar to the preceding turk's head if it is worked without a core. If you are making a knob at the end of a cord, tie it tightly at least 15 cm (6 in.) from the end and spread out the ends into 4 groups, if it is to be a 4 strand knot. But

DIAGRAM 64
Knob knot

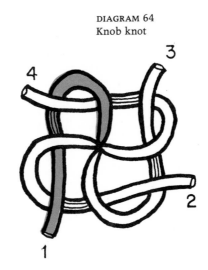

round, which will lie inside the first. Lay 1
anti-clockwise, then 2 over 1, 3 over 2, and
4 over 3 and under 1 to complete the circle.
This is the basic knot, and it is built up as
before by each strand following its neighbouring loop, starting with the lower, or
outer side of the first loop. The very last
threading is down through the centre,
beside the shank or cord, and after the
tightening up, trim closely. The second
key ring tag ends in a knob knot (photograph 35).

if you are making a button, tie a constrictor
knot near the middle of one 30 cm (12 in.)
strand, doubled, forming the loop for the
shank of the button and 2 ends. Thread
the other strand through the shank, at
right angles, also a piece of string to keep
hold of, in case the shank disappears inside
the knot and once again you have 4
working end. Work the knot on your left
hand held out flat palm upwards, with the
string or cord hanging down and held
between first and second fingers, and the 4
strands spread out on your palm. Number
them and working anti-clockwise, lay 1
under 2, 2 under 3, 3 under 4, and 4 under
1, which means threading it up through the
first loop. Make all the loops fairly small
and even before going on to the second

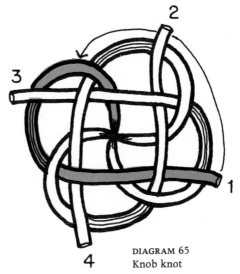

DIAGRAM 65
Knob knot

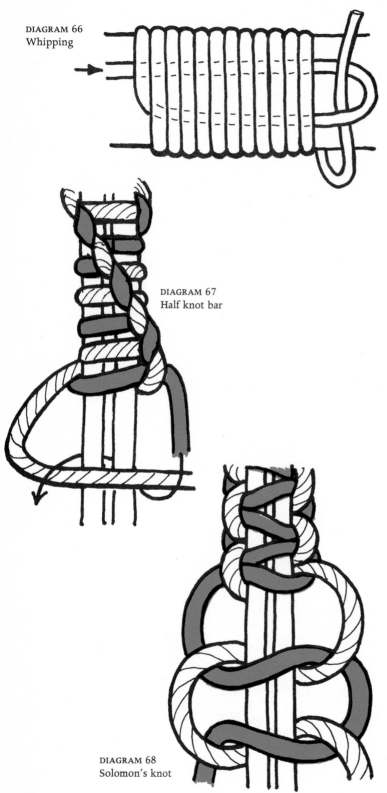

DIAGRAM 66
Whipping

DIAGRAM 67
Half knot bar

DIAGRAM 68
Solomon's knot

(f) A whipping

A simple and useful binding knot. Lay a loop along the core to be covered, and wrap it closely and firmly with one end, working towards the loop. Push the working end through the loop and pull on the other end until the loop disappears. Trim the ends.

(g) Square knotting

This is a combination of two knots, used independently or together to produce solid bars or fabrics, the half knot and the half hitch.

THE HALF KNOT   This is usually worked with groups of 4 strands, 2 workers and 2 for the core. Pin the strands to the board and lay the left hand worker over the core, in the shape of a 4. Take the right hand worker over the first end, round the back of the core and out through the loop of the 4. Tighten up. If this is repeated, it will form a spiral line running round the core.

Solomon's knot   If the half knot is followed by a half knot started from the right (forming a reverse 4), the result will be a square, or Solomon's knot, which looks like a reef knot round a core. A succession of these will form a bar, or several groups of 4 strands can be set up, and after one row of knots, the next row of knots is staggered by starting it after the first 2 strands. The third row starts at the beginning again, and the rows continue alternating to make a fabric, close or open according to the spacing of the rows. The pot stand (photograph 39) is made up of 4 groups of 4 thick iris leaves, doubled, worked into 7 rows of alternating square knots. Each corner knot was then undone, and the ends gathered into 4 corner bundles, held by a whipping of a twisted leaf.

THE HALF HITCH   In diagram 69, the half hitch has been worked with the same strand. This has produced a clove hitch, or cording knot. If the hitching is continued tightly with the same strand, it will form a spiral similar to the half knot spiral. For the knot to lie flat, the half hitch is followed by a reverse half hitch, as in tatting (diagram 70). The frame of the wall hanging in photograph 40 is covered with half hitches in groups of 3, worked with leaves from the outside and fillis string from the inside of the frame. The wall hanging itself contains a variety of knots and plaits as well as some canvas type stitches, using iris siberica as thread on a piece of chair caning in place of canvas.

On a very different scale, delicate embroidery has been worked by stitching straws and grasses into a background of fine net, in photograph 41. The fragment came from a nineteenth-century dress which may have belonged to the Empress Eugenie.

DIAGRAM 69
Half hitch

DIAGRAM 70
Half hitch and reverse half hitch

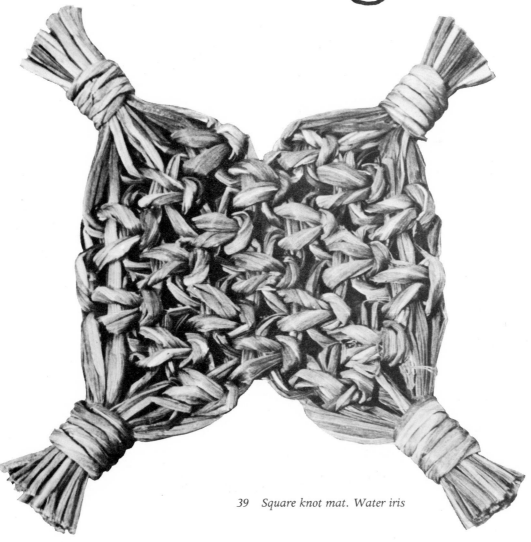

39   Square knot mat. Water iris

*40 Wallhanging in a variety of
iris leaves, reeds, and soft stems,
using plaiting, knotting, corn-dolly
and canvas-work techniques on
chair cane and hessian background.
The frame is bound in alternating
groups of half hitches in twisted
iris leaves and fillis string*

*41 Embroidered fragment of
nineteenth century dress*

9 Marquetry and other uses

USING LEAVES AS A VENEER

If you look closely at a single dried iris or montbretia leaf you will see how much it differs from the tip to the base, and from one side to the other. Collect some leaves carefully from different plants through the seasons and at different stages of growth, so that you have a variety to choose from. After pressing, or ironing flat, they can be sorted into a surprisingly wide range of colours and textures, and used like veneers of different woods. The colours vary from the white of sweet corn sheaths, through yellow tan and green to brown and purple as well as varying from matt surfaces to the shiny inner surface of a leaf close to the base of a flower stem, and the silver inside the fold at the foot of an iris leaf.

A simple idea is to cover a given area entirely with leaves, cut out a design, and mount it on a contrasting background. The design in photograph 42 was a silhouette taken from a photograph of Sri Lanka fishermen perched on poles. It was drawn on tracing paper and then covered with strips of leaves laid horizontally, using an adhesive such as *Evostick Timebond*, which allows a certain amount of adjusting. The change of colour in the bottom left hand corner is where the fold of the iris leaf starts, and helped to give a feeling of water. Turning over to the paper side where the drawing was visible the shapes, being rather intricate, were cut with a very sharp pointed blade, through the paper and leaves onto a soft strawboard, in short jabs rather than long strokes. To give some life to the dark figures, instead of glueing the cut out picture straight onto the suede backing, it was stuck first to a sheet of non-reflective glass, allowing shadows to form at the edges. As the edges of the picture need protection, a cardboard frame was built up to a suitable height and glued onto a backing board before it was covered, and the picture inserted. Having cut out the little figures, it seemed a pity not to

use them, so a reverse picture was soon mounted, with a few extra leaves added. Photograph 43.

The box lid, shown in photograph 44, was done differently, with each leaf section inserted separately into the design, like marquetry. For this you will need to draw the design twice on tracing paper, one to be used as the base of the picture, and the other to be cut out. Starting at one edge, glue a piece of leaf onto one section at a time, following the direction of the design with the grain of the leaf. Turn the paper over and cut out the section from the back, where the design shows through, and then

42   *Cut out panel. Iris, montbretia, day lily*

glue it to the corresponding position on the complete sheet. Work gradually over the picture, matching the leaves to the intention of the design, and pressing it under a weight at intervals. As the two pictures are identical the various pieces should fit together like a jigsaw puzzle, but care and a very sharp craft knife will be needed. When complete, a thin layer of varnish or *Scotchguard* may be applied. A frame was made as before, and fixed to the box lid after covering, and inserting the picture.

Sometimes, when a leaf is being ironed, it will curl itself up into a circle. This happened with the base of pampas grass leaves, and was a convenient way of getting the circular bubbles for the mobile in photograph 13.

44 *Box lid covered in reed mace, iris, montbretia, day lily, crocosmia*

COVERING A BOOK

This can be done with very flat leaves of even width, such as reed mace. The top half of each leaf was used for the book shown in photograph 45 being the thinner part of the leaf. Two different lengths will be needed, as in a rectangular mat. The long ones go right round the book from edge to edge, so if the book is 12 cm (5 in.) wide cut them about 40 cm (16 in.) long, to allow for the overlaps inside, the spine, and the 'take up' during the weaving. For short lengths, measure the height of the book plus 4 cm at either end.

Glue the ends of the longer leaves to the front inside edge of the stiff cover, keeping them very close to each other, then bend them over the edge to lie on top of the cover towards the back of the book. Weave the short ends across closely, in check or twill weave, glueing each end down inside the cover at either end as soon as it is woven. Carry on round the book, sliding a film of glue under a finished section of weaving, and turning the book over to complete the back. Fold the ends of the leaves over the edge of the back cover and glue down inside. Neaten the inside by covering with suitable endpapers – the hand made paper of leaves (photograph 51) was used inside the book illustrated.

CORN DOLLY SPIRAL

Country people often used to make babies rattles from rushes, using a corn dolly spiral. The method can comfortably be used on any number of strands from 4 to 9, and while the rattles are usually worked with 7, it is much easier to learn on 5, which gives a square shape in the middle. Practice if you can on the common rush (*juncus communis*) which grows 50 to 100 cm (18 to 32 in.) long in marshy ground throughout Britain and is easy to use, being similar in size and texture to straw. The material needs to be damped and mellowed just enough to bend without cracking, but without being limp. This is one of the few times that you don't wipe the rushes firmly,

as they have to be kept round, not flattened. At first, work round a core, such as a pencil, piece of dowelling or thick knitting needle, to learn the movement while the size of the spiral stays the same (photograph 46).

Choose 5 rushes the same thickness but different lengths, so that the joins will be staggered, cut off the flowers and thin tips, and tie the tips to the foot of the core, spreading out the strands to N, W, S, with two to E. Take the E nearest you straight over to N, without a bend, but touching the core on the way, so it will lie slightly over N. Hold these two strands lightly and turn the work a quarter turn to the right, replacing the left thumb just over the first fold, to hold it in place. Bend N closely

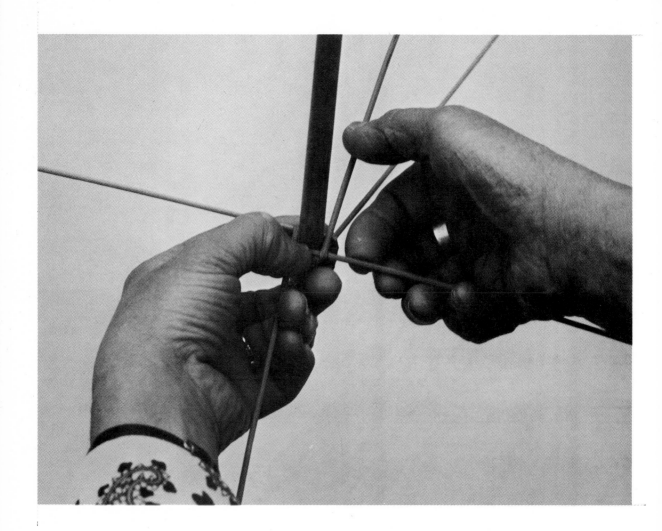

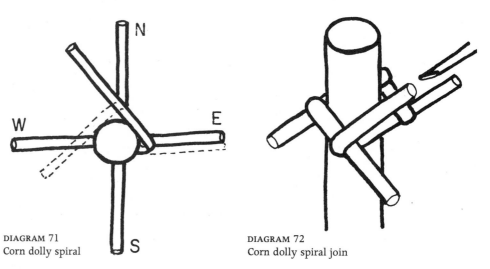

DIAGRAM 71
Corn dolly spiral

DIAGRAM 72
Corn dolly spiral join

up and over E, touch the core and lay it across W; turn the work in the same way, fold W closely up and over N and lay it across S. The work continues in this way, keeping the folds close and even, but the sections in between round and unsquashed.

TO JOIN: near the end of a strand, or before if it begins to feel woody, cut the old strand just past a corner, after it has been folded over the previous corner as usual, and make a space inside it with a thick needle for at least 1 cm ($\frac{1}{2}$ in.). Choose a suitable new rush, trim the tip and insert it as far as it will go, and the next movement should cover the join. You can make a long length of even spiral by gradually withdrawing the core as it gets covered, so that it is continually in use as a gauge. Remove the core and tie off, and the plait can be gently bent into a curve while damp. If the ends are brought together and stitched behind the centre, this can be made into a hair ornament with the addition of a polished length of pointed wood or bamboo to hold it in place.

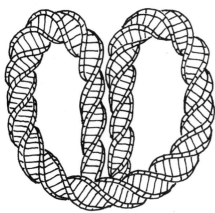

DIAGRAM 73
Corn dolly hair
ornament

Rattle

This can be done with 7 rushes of a thicker and longer variety without a join. Tie them tightly together, 10 or 15 cm (4 or 6 in.) from the butt ends and again at the butts. This will be held like the previous core, with the other ends of the rushes spread out to 6 positions instead of 4, but this time the spiral will increase and decrease in size. Take each rush up to its neighbour as before, but instead of crossing it, lay the one in your hand on the right of, but touching, its neighbour. If you do this each time, the central figure, a hexagon now, not a square, will increase rapidly. When it is 5 cm (2 in.) across, start to shape the rattle by crossing over the corner each time. This will bring it in, by making the hexagon smaller. Practice will soon show you how to regulate the shape by the amount you cross over the corner. You can either cut out the core, and end up with a little plait (photograph 47), or use some of it as a solid core to make a firm handle.

47 *Rush rattle*

Tie off the ends, which may be threaded in with a needle while still damp, after being flattened. Remember to insert a bell before the opening becomes too small.

BRUSHES

These are easily made from bundles of leaves or the small common rush. The brush in photograph 48 was made from a bundle 50 cm (18 in.) long, plaited for about 15 cm (6 in.) in the middle, bent over and tied together firmly with a constrictor knot. Another bundle was pushed through the loop formed, bent down on either side and tied all round again. The strands are bound together with a small plait or rope, in the form of a whipping. If you want a flatter brush, after tying all the strands together splay out the bundle to flatten, divide it into groups, and pair right across once or twice, using a group as one stake.

To give the brush a wooden handle, group the strands evenly round the end of the handle and tie very tightly in at least two places before binding and trimming.

GRASS SKIRT

Worked on the same lines as a full size grass skirt, the doll's skirt in photograph 49 is made of crocus leaves.

Start by making a fine plait or rope, long enough to tie round the waist, knot it at each end, and stretch it out by pinning it to a soft board, through the knots. Damp and straighten the leaves, and picking up a small bundle at a time, bend it into a U fold in the middle. Push the loop under the plait, draw the ends of the bundle through the loop and tighten up into a firm hitch. Repeat all the way along, pushing the little bundles close together until there are enough to encircle the waist. Turn the skirt upside down, bend a strong leaf round the first bunch to give 2 working ends, and pair right across to keep the leaves in position. This can be repeated, and the ends of the pairing rows can also be used as tying ends.

The skirt can be decorated with shells or flowers. To make flowers, the damp leaves of sweetcorn husks are pliable and easy to use. Cut sections right across the leaves, roll one or two into a tight tube the size of a pencil, tie very tightly (constrictor knot) with a linen thread and cut close to the tie on one side. While damp,

49   *Doll's grass skirt. Crocus leaves.*
Flowers of sweet corn

Loom weaving

the petals on the other side are pressed
away from the centre, after shredding
them with a needle. The ends of the knot
can be used to sew the flower to the skirt.

LOOM WEAVING

Fabric can be woven on a loom using a
strong warp of cotton or linen and using
leaves or rushes in the weft, either on their
own or combined with threads. The rushes
and leaves can be used in short lengths or
bent over at the edges to form a continuous weft, adding in new material when
necessary, to keep the thickness as even
as possible. They need to be damped and
mellowed before use, and should be beaten
back very hard indeed. The warp ends are
usually spaced out in dense groups, to
contrast with the texture of the rushes or
leaves and keep them firmly in place. If
the strands are to be used in short lengths,
the edges are trimmed after the work is

taken off the loom. A wide loom could make use of longer lengths, and the material can be cut between two warp sections into small mats, if necessary.

The mats are heatproof, hardwearing and washable, but should be dried off fairly quickly to prevent mould spots appearing.

In the mat in photograph 50 some of the rushes have been dyed black to give a more pronounced design.

IO Making paper

If the plant material that you have gathered has been damaged beyond normal use or kept so long that it has lost its 'body', it can still be put to good use by turning it into pulp and making paper with an unusual texture.

In India, writing has been done directly onto palm leaves, which were then turned into books by threading a cord through a hole in one end of each leaf. In Egypt, the stems of the 3 m (3 yd) tall papyrus were used for papermaking. They were split into long strips which were laid side by side and then covered with another layer of strips laid at right angles to the first. Pressure was applied, probably by hitting a wooden block as it was placed over different sections, and then smoothing the whole surface with a very flat stone or bone.

Paper as we know it today originated in China about AD100. The basic ingredients are the cellulose fibres to be found in most plants, which have the property of swelling in water and sticking together when the water has drained away or been squeezed out. We can regulate the thickness of the paper by the amount of pulp in the water, and the texture by the type of fibre and the way we have previously treated it. Commercially, the pulp is usually made of wood, cotton, straw or esparto grass, but leaves of all the types we have used so far, the rushes, reeds and similar plants all provide usable fibres. You can begin with the dry material, or allow it to start rotting first. A certain amount of mould spotting on the white sweetcorn sheath leaves can produce an interesting grey paper. Start by cutting it all up into lengths of about 2 cm (1 in.) and then to remove the non-fibrous tissues boil it in a solution of caustic soda (2 dessertspoons to 1 litre – $1\frac{3}{4}$ pints) for at least two hours till the fibres are free. Wash in a sieve to remove the waste and soda, and then in a cloth under a running tap to cleanse really well. Pounding with a wooden mallet will help to separate the fibres into finer strands and make for a smoother paper. The pulp can be bleached with a solution of household bleach overnight, and after washing out it is ready for use.

Moulds

To make sheets of paper, some sort of a mould will be needed. This can be anything from a bamboo table mat to a proper paper-making mould, complete with removable deckle, which is a raised edge to hold the pulp. However it is quite easy to make a simple frame. The wood is preferably straight grained mahogany, or another wood which will stand up to the continual wetting and drying, and the joints dovetailed and glued. The surface is covered with a woven wire fabric or terylene mesh or perforated zinc, tacked firmly along the sides with rustless nails. If the surface can be made rigid and slightly convex, it should be possible to couch the pulp, that is, turn it over and transfer it to a blanket, so that the mould can be reused at once. If not, the pulp is left to dry on the mould.

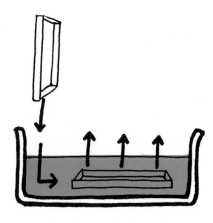

DIAGRAM 74
Hand made paper

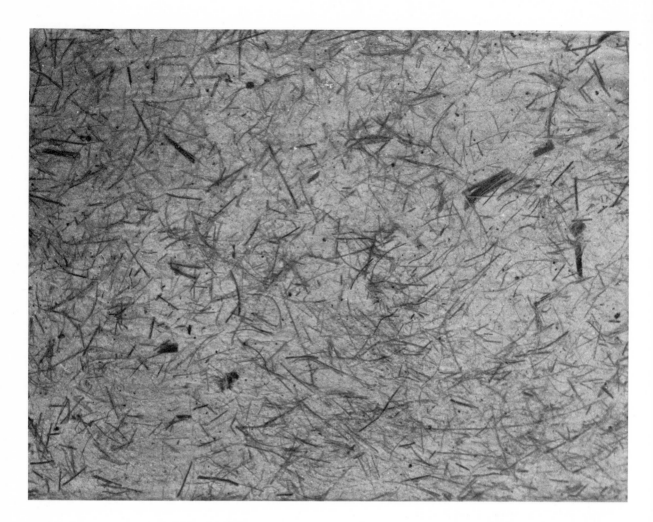

Making the sheets

Nothing with an iron content should come into contact with the pulp, or stains will result. The pulp is mixed with hot water in a container big enough to allow easy movement of the frame in the liquid. The mixture will look like thin soup, and as sheets are taken out more pulp is added to keep the consistency right. The frame is held by the side, vertically, lowered into the pulp, and the bottom edge is raised to a horizontal position as the mould is lifted out. The water drains away, leaving a layer of pulp on the surface. If it looks uneven, turn the frame upside down onto the surface of the water and the pulp will float off to be reused. Try again until the sheet of pulp looks satisfactory, then either leave it to dry completely before removing it from the mould, or couch it at once onto a saturated piece of springy, felted woollen blanket, by pressing the mould with a smooth rocking movement from one side to the other. Lay another blanket on top and repeat several times to build up a 'post'. There should be extra blankets at the top and bottom of the pile as well as a rigid board, and the post is then pressed to remove the excess water. Carefully peel off the blankets and lift the paper by two corners and put it to dry, either by hanging it over a thick cord, or laying it on an open weave cloth, such as scrim, stretched on a frame. The paper then needs time to mature, being pressed and aired and turned occasionally. If necessary, after a fortnight, to make the paper less absorbent, it can be sized by painting with a solution of gelatine (30 gr to 2 litres – 1 oz to 3 pints of water for a light size). Press between blotting paper and dry again, turning at intervals.

You can use pulp from one plant or a mixture of several, and if you want to add wood pulp, some egg boxes, torn up, soaked, and put through a liquidizer, are a convenient source of supply. Cotton or linen rags can be added, and make very good quality paper, but they need a lot of boiling and liquidizing.

Papers made from different leaves will have a variety of colours and textures and the unusual, uneven edge is in itself attractive. It is very suitable to use as endpapers for a book covered with woven reed mace.

These are only some of the possibilities of leaves and rushes. Over the centuries and throughout the world, different plants and changing needs have produced an endless variety of ways to use them. The soft fibres do not usually survive great lapses of time but the dry sands of Egypt have preserved some fine examples, like the cosmetic box and the elaborate sandal of palm leaves, dating from about 1300 BC. (Photograph 52).

The reference museum at Kew Gardens contains a much more recent pair of beautifully shaped slippers – using the local material of an English coast, they are made of coiled marram grass.

Where large quantities of suitable material are available, things have been produced on a much bigger scale for all sorts of domestic purposes, including quite often complete houses. Palm leaves are plaited while still attached to the main rib to make roofing 'tiles' and fill in walls – hurricanes can blow through these houses, or, if they are destroyed, they can be rebuilt in a few hours. But the Ma'dan homes in the marshes of Southern Iraq are quite different in structure: made from great arching bundles of rushes some are almost like palaces, and it may take 150 men three weeks to put one up.

However, living on reed islands in lake Titicaca, the Peruvian Indians seem to have used the plant to the utmost: building houses, making mattresses, burning it as fuel and tying it into seaworthy boats capable of crossing the Atlantic, as Thor Heyerdahl demonstrated with his reed boat *Ra*. So what we do with our material depends on us – the possibilities are there for exploring, and all the pleasure of creating.

52   Ancient Egyptian sandal. Palm leaf
The British Museum, London

Bibliography

The Ashley Book of Knots, Faber and Faber, 1947

Rushwork, Roffey and Cross, Pitman, 1952

Introducing Rushcraft, K. Whitbourn, Batsford, 1969

Rushwork, N. Florence, Bell and Sons, 1962

Indian Basket Weaving, The Navajo School of Indian Basketry, Dover Publications Inc, New York, 1971

A Golden Dolly, M. Lambeth, John Baker, 1969

The Craft of Straw Decoration, Alec Coker, Dryad Press, 1971

Papermaking, The Technical Section of the Papermakers Association, Surrey, 1949

Papermaking as an Artistic Craft, John Mason, Faber and Faber, 1959

One Hundred and Fifty Years of Papermaking by Hand, Maidstone, 1960

Strawwork and Corn Dollies, Lettice Sandford, Batsford, 1974

Baskets as Textile Art, Ed Rossbach, Studio Vista, 1975

Techniques of Basketry, Virginia Harvey, Batsford, 1975

Suppliers

Great Britain

Rushes
Tom Metcalfe Arnold
Holywell, St Ives
Huntingdon

Debenham Rush Weavers
Debenham, Suffolk

Dryad (Reeves) Ltd
Northgates, Leicester

Needles
Available from most drapers or
department stores. *Milwards
Repair Kit* contains the ideal
needles.

Funnel
Obtainable from hardware shops in
all sizes. The plastic ones are the
best for the purpose of this craft
A suitable funnel can be made
from the top of a plastic bottle

Soft gardening string
Supplied by all gardening shops
and most hardware stores

USA

Naturalcraft
2199 Bancroft Way
Berkeley
California 94704

Cane & Basket Supply Co
1283 South Cochran Avenue
Los Angeles
California 90019

Triarco Arts & Crafts
7330 North Clark Street
Chicago
Illinois 60626
(write for address of
outlet nearest you)

Earth Guild/Grateful Union
Mail Order Service
149 Putnam Avenue
Cambridge
Massachusetts 02139

Peerless Rattan & Reed
97 Washington Street
New York
New York 10006

The Workshop
Box 158
Pittsford
New York 14534

Billy Arthur Inc
University Mall
Chapel Hill
North Carolina 27514

Sax Arts & Crafts
Box 2002
Milwaukee
Wisconsin 53201

List of photographs